RECOLLECTIONS OF THE CAMPAIGN

IN

MALWA AND CENTRAL INDIA

UNDER

MAJOR GENERAL SIR HUGH ROSE, G. C. B.

RECOLLECTIONS OF THE CAMPAIGN

IN

MALWA AND CENTRAL INDIA

UNDER

MAJOR GENERAL SIR HUGH ROSE, G. C. B.

BY

ASSISTANT SURGEON JOHN HENRY
SYLVESTER, F.G.S.

GYAN

Published by

Gyan Publishing House
5, Ansari Road
Daryaganj, New Delhi-110002
Phone: 011-47034999, 9811692060
E-mail: books@gyanbooks.com

Distribution Network
gyanbooks.com
India, USA, Canada, UK, Australia, France

ISBN: 978-81-212-7097-7 (PB)
First Published, 1860

2nd Impression 2024

Printed at: Gyan Press, Delhi.

RECOLLECTIONS OF THE CAMPAIGN IN MALWA AND CENTRAL INDIA UNDER MAJOR GENERAL SIR HUGH ROSE, G. C. B.

Author: JOHN HENRY SYLVESTER

RECOLLECTIONS OF THE CAMPAIGN

IN

MALWA AND CENTRAL INDIA

UNDER

MAJOR GENERAL SIR HUGH ROSE, G.C.B.,

BY

ASSISTANT SURGEON JOHN HENRY SYLVESTER, F.G.S.,

ASSOCIATE OF KING'S COLLEGE, &c.,

2nd REGIMENT MAYNE'S HORSE.

Forsan et hæc olim meminisse juvabit. Œn: lib. i.

BOMBAY: SMITH, TAYLOR, & CO.

1860.

THESE Recollections of the Campaign in Malwa and Central India, written from time to time while in pursuit of Tantia Topee and his rebel hordes, originally appeared in the columns of the *Bombay Standard*, but now with the addition of the final pursuit and capture of the Rebel Chief, and with a more detailed account of some of the principal features of the Campaign, are dedicated by kind permission with feelings of the most sincere respect to Major-General Sir Hugh Rose, G.C.B.,

By his obliged servant,

THE AUTHOR.

Camp Birseeah, May 1860.

CONTENTS.

CHAPTER IV.

CHAPTER V.

CHAPTER VI.

CHAPTER VII.

CHAPTER VIII.

CHAPTER IX.

CHAPTER X.

CHAPTER XI.

CHAPTER XII.

CHAPTER XIII.

CHAPTER XIV.

RECOLLECTIONS,

&c.

FIRST INTELLIGENCE OF THE MUTINY—THE 14TH DRAGOONS AND 25TH REGT. MARCH ON AHMEDNUGGUR, THROUGH RAIN AND MUD—DISAFFECTION OF THE HYDRABAD CONTINGENT, AT AURUNGABAD—THE MUTINY THERE SUPPRESSED—A FIELD FORCE MARCHES INTO BERAR.

THE Treaty of Peace with Persia had scarcely been promulgated to the Force under Sir James Outram, when the transport ships commenced bringing our troops back to Bombay. Amongst the first to arrive were H. M.'s 14th Light Dragoons, who marched to their old quarters at Kirkee, gladly welcoming the change from the hot and barren sands of Persia to their comfortable quarters in cantonment. They were, however, fated to enjoy them for a few days only; and, growing tired of the monotony of a dragoon's life in time of peace, responded to the trumpet call of "Boot and Saddle!" with unusual alacrity, as the shrill notes echoed through their lines at midnight on the 9th of June 1857. The moon lit up the night as they wound their way along the hot and dusty roads towards Poona, and bade farewell to their wives, children, and comrades, who followed them, wishing to put off the moment of separation as long as possible. The band struck up "The girl I left behind me," and amidst thousands of well-wishes and tender farewells, mingled with injunctions of a less peaceful nature, such as "Give 'em one for me, Bill!" we left all trace of dwellings behind, and took the road to Loonee.

Now the gigantic mutiny was yet in embryo, and its first tidings came dropping like the pop-popping of skirmishers in the beginning of an action, but each piece of intelligence more serious than the last, and with each instalment the blood of this gallant band of Englishmen grew warmer, and more anxious to avenge their countrymen so cowardly and basely murdered. And little thought they then how soon their wishes would be gratified: they knew not whither they were bound, and cared less, so long as it was onward, where their brother soldiers were fighting for life, beleaguered by numbers in proportion of a thousand to one.

On our second day's march we were joined by what was then considered a most questionable reinforcement, the Bombay 25th Regiment of Native Infantry, commanded by Major Follett. I need not now, after their brilliant services under that most intelligent and very superior officer and tactician, say how unfounded were all our doubts of their loyalty. Still, with daily intelligence of mutinies among the staunch and petted Regiments of Bengal, it was but human to doubt the Asiatic race. Thus the 14th Dragoons and 5th Native Infantry, with small sympathy between them, and under command of Major-General Woodburn, C.B., marched on Ahmednuggur, and it was these two corps that formed the nucleus of that Force which, if it has not duly received, has *earned* one of the brightest names in the annals of Eastern warfare, and had the grand fortune to be commanded by our most dashing and never-defeated English General, Sir Hugh Rose, G.C.B. But before his advent, much was to be done. The Nizam's dominions wanted but the match applied, to rouse the seething mass into a conflagration which would have swept through Behar and the Nagpoor territory.

On the third day of the march of our small Force, the monsoon burst in full strength over us, just as we left Seeroor, and by the time our halting-place was reached the darkness and rain were thick and heavy, the black cotton soil was knee-deep in mud, so that the horses could not be kept at their pickets, and dashed about in the darkness like so many wild ones; and the men whose tents and baggage had not arrived, got shelter as they best could, and, soaked through cloak and tunic, hailed the daylight, and order to march again, with something like satisfaction. Thus, battling with rain and mud, with the worst of carriage for our baggage, which had to be dragged over the worst of roads, and in the worst of seasons, for as yet rebel leaders had not taught us the value of animal transport, and limited baggage, we reached Ahmednugger. The Brigadier here was importuned by Civilians on all sides to send troops. Each thought his district in greatest need, and all were equally anxious to save it, and prevent an outbreak. It was here we first heard the smothered growl of disaffection among the troops at Aurungabad, and the jeopardy of the garrison at Mhow. The danger at this latter place was considered the most imminent, so that we proceeded in the direction of Malligaum *en route*, only to be recalled immediately to proceed to Aurungabad. False reports of the "Fall of Delhi," with fabulous numbers reported killed, came in every few days only to be contradicted, but they were generally believed, as no one at that time ever imagined the gigantic scale the mutiny afterwards assumed, and sanguine officers were willing to bet they should never "see a shot fired."

On the 19th of June Captain H. O. Mayne arrived, with the ladies and children, from Aurungabad, and with such other tidings as induced the Major-General to march at once on that station; our force having the very acceptable reinforcement of the 4th Battalion 2d Company Bombay Artillery, manned by Europeans and commanded by Major Woolcombe, C.B. The roads were vile, and the Godavery river girth deep, but we did not stay to pitch our tents, and merely halted to feed and give the Infantry and horses rest. The men were so overpowered by sleep that we halted from 11 P. M. till 3 A.M., on the road side, near Dygaon. Here, lining the road, the whole Force was to be seen fast asleep, without the slightest shelter, and the rain pouring steadily down on them.

At 10 A.M. on the morning of the 23rd, we reached our destination, and were joined by Captain Abbott and other officers of the Contingent, who had remained in the mess-house with those officers and men of the 1st Regiment of Cavalry who were trustworthy, and it was with the faithless of these corps that we had to deal. They were encamped on high ground beyond the cantonment on the Jaulna road. Our column proceeded there, and formed up, the Battery with 25th Regiment in square on its right flank, one squadron of Dragoons on its left, the remaining squadron in its rear. The Major General and Staff now proceeded to the front, and ordered the men of the Contingent to parade, which for the most part they did, and mild measures were resorted to to induce them to return to their allegiance. Many did so, but one native officer, seeing so many going against his cause, summarily ended the affair by discharging his pistol at Captain Abbott, which brought a shot in return. Neither of the missiles took effect, though but a few paces separated officer and trooper. The Brigadier now gave the order to open fire, and pour grape upon the troopers, who had all flown to their horses, ready saddled, in the lines; but unluckily the guns each had a nine-pounder shot in them, and these had first to be shot out, and now the mutineers were in full flight, and the 14th Dragoons were ordered to pursue. Captain Gall led his Troop after those escaping by the Jaulna road, and Captain Barrett followed the few who took the open country, Captain Abbott and some loyal sowars joining in pursuit. Few were overtaken, the tired horses of the Regulars, so heavily laden, being unable to catch the fresh, lightly-mounted cattle of the mutineers. I have no doubt Brigadier Woodburn was led to believe that the men simply required a little pacification, and they would return to their duty. In order to prevent any disturbance in the Cantonment among the Native Infantry and Artillery, two guns, two Companies of the 25th Regiment, some Madras Sappers and Miners, and Dragoons, all under command of Lieutenant Leith, were judiciously placed near the bridge over the river leading to the Cavalry lines.

This affair having been disposed of, and the prisoners marched into Camp, Courts Martial immediately commenced. The first prisoner tried was Meer Fider Ali, who attempted to prove an *alibi*, but the following day the whole of the troops in the station, including the Contingent, were paraded to see him hanged. This was done by placing him on a cart, which, after the adjustment of the noose, was driven from beneath him, and the whole Force present were marched past that they might have an uninterrupted view. That evening a Squadron of the 14th Dragoons, two of Woolcombe's guns, two of the Nizam's, as well as some Contingent and Bombay Native Infantry, all under command of Captain Gall, marched at dusk on Boldana in Berar, as there was a large sum of money in the treasury there, guarded by a troop of this mutinous corps of the Nizam's.

We fell in at dusk that night, according to order, and provided ourselves with torches and guides to find our way; but as there existed but a mere track across country, we soon lost that and got fairly into the fields, and were obliged finally to pull up, and then officers were to be seen groping about, endeavouring to find the road again. This accomplished, we marched all night, resting occasionally for an hour or so; and being ordered to make forced marches we never pitched tents, but simply encamped, when tired and hot, under magnificent trees, which were in great plenty, and on the third day we reached Boldana, a distance of nearly one hundred miles. There was not a single officer or soldier who was not drenched to the skin, as all had passed the previous night in pouring rain, without shelter of any kind. We sat round bonfires of curby stalks, exhibiting a sort of Pecksniffian jollity, and, thanks to six enterprising dhooly-bearers, we were not entirely reduced to captain's biscuits: they had brought us some uncooked meat, bread, and pale ale, and by furnishing the usual parole of "dead man" when there was a probability of the dhooly being required to carry a sick one, it reached us intact; and though we had no knives, forks, or plates, each placed on a stick sufficient meat for his wants, and toasted it in the flames. Then, sleeping with our backs to the fire, on the wet ground, we awaited morning, and marched into the bleak-looking cantonment of Boldana. On gaining the Residency, we found the Resident had already disarmed the troop of Cavalry, and left us nought to do but escort the troopers back as prisoners. Twenty thousand men were reported to be in readiness to take arms against Government in this one district alone, and we did not envy the position of the hospitable Resident, who had to remain almost alone here, with a few Bheel policemen as a guard.

The rain had abated somewhat of its former violence, and a despatch from General Woodburn recalled us with all haste. We returned through a splendid tract of undulating country, covered with flowering shrubs and abounding with antelope, which we often saw in immense herds. We passed through the towns of Jaffarabad and Jaulna, in order to create a demonstration. The 6th Madras Light Cavalry were stationed at the latter place, and received the officers of our Force with unbounded hospitality, commencing with a luxurious breakfast on our arrival, which was at near midday: but we had had so little rest, that some ten or twelve of us fell asleep at the table ere the meal had well commenced, and our faces were so scorched by the sun that scarce one of us could venture an ablution without considerable suffering. On the 6th of July, we rejoined the head quarters of the Force, our Infantry worn out and footsore, and nearly the whole company of Bombay Sappers and Miners who accompanied us required to be carried. When within sight of the tents of the Force we were provokingly halted, and told we had to march towards Mhow on the morrow, whereas we looked for at least a night or so in bed. One of the dragoons, who heard we were to be off again, delivered himself of the following exclamation —" I say, Harry, I'm blowed if old G—— hasn't bin and discovered perpetual motion."

The Brigadier had not been idle in our absence, but had promptly and vigorously carried out the sentences of the Courts Martial on the prisoners, and we arrived in time to witness some of the executions: some were blown from the cannon's mouth, others shot with carbines. They met their fate as none other than fanatics could, and doubtless saw Paradise in the shadow of our guns, though it struck me a shudder passed through their dusky frames as their bared chests touched the cold metal of the guns. A word and a flash blew the head high in mid-air, without so much as displacement of the bandage from the eyes, the arms flew wide asunder, the legs beneath the gun, and the chest, to fill the vacuum caused by the explosion, was driven back, bespattering gun and gunners.

CHAPTER II.

THE DEKKAN FIELD FORCE MARCHES TO THE RELIEF OF MHOW—DISARMS MUTINOUS TROOPS AT ASSEERGHÚR—ARRIVES IN MHOW—THE FORCE IS INCREASED, AND MARCHES ON FORT DHAR, UNDER THE NAME OF THE MALWA FIELD FORCE—OPERATIONS BEFORE FORT DHAR—CAPTURE OF THE FORTRESS.

General Woodburn's ill health compelled him to give up command of the Force, and Major Follett, of the 25th Regiment, succeeded him. On the 9th of July the tidings of the Mhow and Indore mutinies reached us, and on the 12th we marched on those places, leaving behind 50 sabres of H. M. 14th Dragoons for the protection of the station.

It has been said, that had we marched on Mhow at once, instead of going into the Berar Valley, the mutinies at Mhow and Indore would never have occurred. Government, however, entirely suppressed the rebellion in the Dekkan by the course taken, and could never have reached Mhow in time. Besides which, the 1st Bengal Cavalry and 23rd Regiment B. N. I., stationed there, told their officers that they should leave them and go to Delhi so soon as they received intelligence of European Troops coming near them: and therefore, had the Dekkan Field Force marched earlier on Mhow it would only have hastened the outbreak. It was not generally known, either, that we had to pass through the Asseerghur jungles, which were closed to troops by Government orders from the months of June to November, as being considered fatal to Europeans, rife as they then are with malaria. Nevertheless, in spite of the jokes at our expense, that we were going to Mhow by water, &c., we started only too gladly to the relief of the Europeans in jeopardy, and shut up in the fort there. As we passed through the deadly valley of the Taptee we made the acquaintance of Malaria's eldest son, cholera: it appeared first amongst the Dragoons at Edulabad, and at Antoolee many of the sepoys of the 25th Regt. died. Major Follett, temporarily commanding the Force, was seized also, and died that evening. We tried to march away from it, but it would not leave us, and poor Major Follett's remains were carried on and buried at Burhampoor. The funerals, every evening, of the victims began to get disheartening, and threw a gloom over the camp. At Asseerghur, Brigadier, now Sir Charles Stuart, commenced his fortunate command. Captain Keatinge, Political Agent for Nemar, joined us at Burhampoor, and introduced us to a mutinous company of Gwalior Infantry, which was disarmed, and the men were allowed to proceed wherever it pleased them, which was doubtless to take arms against us in Hindustan. This was the course pursued in the later days of the campaign—fortunately not very generally at the outset, or we should have had still greater numbers arrayed against us in the ravines of Calpee, and under the death-dealing sun at Koonch, when we were enfeebled by marching and watching, and our ranks weakened by sword, bullet, and disease. At Asseerghur we found other of Scindiah's Infantry who had been disarmed. Drumhead Courts Martial assembled, and three sepoys were executed. Melancholy funeral processions were seen winding out of camp every evening, for cholera continued to make havoc amongst us: the soldiers had to sleep on muddy ground, and were constantly exposed to rain, and the supply of liquor ran short: a sergeant was in charge of the Commissariat Department. At this time Colonel and Mrs. Durand, Dr. Henry Wilson, and some fugitive officers and ladies, having escaped the mutiny at Indore, arrived in our camp. They had suffered much from fatigue, exposure, and other causes. We supplied them with all we could, and Holkar sent the Force thirteen baggage elephants. On the 27th the 14th Dragoons swam across the Nerbudda river: the Infantry, guns, and baggage, crossed at Mokka ka Turr, a ford near Burwai. We then ascended the Vindhya range, 1650 feet, and left, we hoped, all traces and causes of cholera and fever in the Nemar valley beneath us. The climate certainly improved, though the rain fell in torrents. But the huge jungle trees were in their handsomest foliage, and the torrents and cataracts which fell down the gorges in the rocks roared and echoed in the deep gloom of the ravines, for the body of water in the falls was unusual, consequent on the heavy rain.

At Simrool, on the top of the Ghauts, we were joined by the 3rd Regt. of Hydrabad Contingent Cavalry, commanded by Captain P. Orr, and, thus reinforced, we marched into Mhow on the 2nd of August. The Artillery horses were so exhausted, that it became necessary to send for those of the Bengal battery to drag our guns in. We were enthusiastically cheered by those who had been shut up in the fort since the mutiny. The Cantonment was a mass of blackened ruins, save the church and library; the mess-house of the 1st Cavalry was strewn with broken glass, plates, dishes, plated ware, and such articles as were useless to the mutineers: for the outbreak commenced while the officers of that Corps were dining, so that the entire service and dinner were at the disposal of the black troopers. They had taken the green cloth from the billiard table to make a flag, as every one knows the green flag was the emblem of mutiny. Most of the officers had a distance of a mile to run 'ere they gained the Fort, and almost each one ran a narrow escape of his life. Dr. Thornton was saved by concealing himself in a drain until Hungerford's battery guns rumbled over it the next day, when they picked him up, as well the dead bodies of Colonel Platt and the Adjutant, Fegan, both of the 23rd B. N. I. These two officers, having faith in their men, endeavoured to appease them, and met the usual fate of such devotion.

Rain now set in without abatement, and further marching was out of the question: all got shelter as they best could. There were constant alarms in camp, and an uneasy watchfulness was apparent. People said the guns were always loaded, and battery horses saddled: inlying pickets were doubled, and the great men in camp spoke mysteriously. The native element of the Force was stronger than the European, the bazaar was reported full of arms, and men of a fighting cast prowled in numbers about the streets. Holkar's troops at Indore, close by, were in open mutiny, and the Maharajah had, or reported he had, lost all control over them, and confined himself to the upper stories of his palace. Holkar's troops constantly reported they would join the Mhow bazaar, and attack us, and on one occasion so much cannonading was heard in the Indore direction that we believed they were about to do so. The night it occurred was excessively dark We were all dressed and armed, our horses saddled, and in readiness. Every ear was strained to catch the first sound of the enemy's approach, when a dragoon from the picket on the Indore bridge galloped in, and on being challenged replied, as we understood him, "Turn out the picket" (inlying). We were in our saddles in a moment, congratulating ourselves that at last the temerity of the rebels had led them on. Our trumpets had alarmed the whole station: the batteries, H. M.'s 86th, the 25th Regt., and Madras Sappers, had all come to the front. The illusion was dispelled by again questioning the vidette, who replied, he had "come in from the picket," to tell us of the proximity of guns and cannonading, and, disappointed, we unsaddled again.

On the 5th of the month the very refreshing sight of a wing of the 86th Royal County Downs gladdened us. But even Europeans at this crisis proved untrustworthy—some gunners of the Bengal battery robbed the treasure under their care of fourteen thousand rupees. The duty for the Europeans became very severe: they chafed to be led on service, and cast longing eyes on Indore. We will suppose some wise motive kept them away from that city, but we could not learn what. About the commencement of October the monsoon had cleared off. Signs of activity now appeared in every department, especially the Ordnance, in which a siege train was organised, and an officer took charge of the Commissariat; while we were at length roused to activity by reports of Veliattees burning villages not far distant from us, and a force composed of a troop of Dragoons, three companies 25th N. I., two guns, and some Hydrabad Cavalry, all commanded by Major Robertson, proceeded to Maunpoor, in the direction of Dhar.

The field force under Major Robertson was but the advance guard of the Brigade, which was pretty equally divided, one division being commanded by Major Keane, of H. M.'s 86th Regt., the other by the Brigadier. Each left Mhow on the 20th by a different route, for the purpose of clearing Malwa of its rebels, and thus we left a very considerable enemy at Indore in our rear, and reports of dissatisfaction amongst some of the Bombay troops reached us, while 20,000 Gwalior mutineers had threatened to come down and annihilate our small force. Still this bold policy was necessary, and turned out successful, for the Indore troops, instead of coming to the relief of the garrison at Dhar, went off to Hindustan; and at two o'clock on the morning of the 22nd, we made our last march, unmolested, on Fort Dhar. We lost the road, however, and after going nearly two miles on the wrong track, through deep mud and wet nullahs, the mistake was discovered, and our heads turned for Dhar. On the road we joined the Field Force under Major Robertson, which had preceded us, and awaited our arrival at Goozeree.

Captain Mayne, who was attached to the Force, had ridden in advance with some sowars, and returned reporting he had been fired on from the pettah of Fort Dhar, whereupon there was rejoicing at the prospect of approaching hostilities. There was a halt, and the Europeans assembled round the liquor carts, to fortify themselves with what they termed a "morning sneezer." The sepoys, too, plied their brass lotas, and made havoc of the contents of their havresacks. A little rising ground only hid us from the Fort and town.

The 86th Regiment, in skirmishing order,

had no sooner gained the summit, than the booming of guns was heard, announcing that the action had commenced with Major Keane's column, who by another route had come up simultaneously with us, as directed, but on the opposite side of the Fort, with special orders not to engage; but the enemy removed all scruples by engaging him. Our Cavalry and Artillery followed our skirmishers up the rising ground, from which every part of the enemy's position and surrounding country could be seen. Nothing could have been more picturesque, dotted about as this territory is with lakes and trees: between us and the fort was an expanse of water, on the extreme right Major Keane's column in the heat of the engagement, and on our left a series of hills, rocks, and ravines. On one of the eminences the rebels had placed a battery of English nine-pounders, which greeted us with rounds of hammered shot: these in their passage through the air created a most disagreeable whi-r-r-r, while those that fell short in the lake threw up miniature waterspouts. The clusters of the enemy's infantry, too, had scores of many-coloured banners, all lending considerable effect. We formed line, and opened fire on the fort and hill battery, soon disabling one of the guns on the latter position, but the fort proved out of range, and the heavy guns on its bastion were making gaps in our Cavalry ranks. Major Gall, with a troop of Dragoons, was now ordered to charge the hill battery, which he did, and in a few moments the four guns thereon were in our possession, and abandoned to the sepoys of the 25th Regt., who turned them on the enemy and commenced to work them, and the whole line advanced on the ridge of hills which commanded the Fort, though it was beyond the range of all save the Enfield rifles. Major Keane's force on the north side, and the Brigadier on the side nearest the town, had fairly driven in the enemy from his outworks, and the Dragoons and 3rd Nizam's Cavalry dashed in amongst them, cutting up considerable numbers. The former encountered the enemy's Cavalry in swampy ground, where neither could get away: hand-to-hand encounters ensued, which resulted in victory to the dragoon, with perhaps a trifling wound, and death to the rebel—seeming to show that the superiority of swordmanship, so often spoken of as possessed by the Asiatic over the European, does not exist. Many of the semi-savages carried bows and arrows, but they proved very inefficient weapons. One arrow-wound only came to my knowledge, and that scarcely penetrated to any injurious depth.

The enemy still held possession of the town as well as Fort, and the Force, having now warmed to its work, could with difficulty be restrained from storming the former at once. After continued bugling to cease firing, it was assembled and marched into a sort of basin amongst the hills, and encamped, leaving strong pickets and outposts of both Cavalry and Infantry. An irregular fire from the fort was kept up through the day and night. At dark, flaming torches were seen in active movement, and the noise of camels was heard, and doubtless many of the enemy moved off to Mundesoor. On the following day five elephants, and all our Commissariat bullocks, were sent to help to drag in the siege guns, for without them we were helpless against stone walls. Six elephants were seen leaving the fort with a small guard. The Cavalry gave pursuit, overtook themin a village, which was burnt, the elephants brought into camp, and several of their guard killed. The

Commissariat Department was only too glad of such a reinforcement of animal power, and purchased them for the sum of four thousand rupees, which sum the Brigadier—considerately, and on the principle of *bis dat, qui cito dat*—ordered should at once be distributed amongst the 14th and 3rd Hyderabad Cavalry, who captured the creatures. The officers gave up their claim to the men, and it averaged a considerable fraction each. But lo! the Infantry heard of this, and when they saw the Cavalry, cried out, "Who stole the elephants! When *we* storm the Fort, of course you don't expect any prize money." Lucky men| ye Cavalry! Had you never by accident received those rupees, you would never have had aught of the nine lakhs we took from the Treasury. A party of rebels sallied out of the Fort under cover of the jowarree and hemp fields, and set fire to the Government bungalow, which was near the Fort. A mortar battery was thrown up on the height formerly occupied by the rebel battery, and made excellent shell practice into the bastions. On the morning of our third day before the place, the Infantry entered the town, which they occupied without much fighting, the rebels retreating to the fort and pettah. Howitzers were taken into the town, which was held by the 25th Regiment and under command of Major Robertson, who, under a storm of shells from the howitzers into the fort, advanced and took a line of earth-works within 400 yards' distance of the curtains. Behind this the breaching battery was commenced by the Madras Sappers and Miners. The enemy now kept up a constant fire from the embrasures on the men at work, so that the chief part of the operation had to be carried on at night. Companies of Infantry blazed away constantly in return, and the tall chakos with white covers worn by the Royal County Downs were greatly attractive to the matchlockmen. Putting one on a stick, and hoisting it above the earth-work, was always followed by a hail of bullets. They did not work their heavy guns, except at very long intervals, and it was surmised their large ammunition had run short, which was further confirmed by our unburst shells being occasionally returned to us, making a noise as of a monster humming-top. In the meantime the Cavalry had been placed on the roads leading from Dhar to prevent the escape of the garrison, and our siege guns had arrived. And twice at night had Lieuts. Strutt and Christie, with some gunners, fired the pettah, which, being for the most part composed of grass and wood-built houses, burnt and blazed furiously, lighting the town and fort and country for miles. On another occasion a company of the 25th Regiment entered the pettah under cover of the darkness, to complete its destruction. The enemy made a sortie on these occasions: the small-arm firing was fast and furious, but to small effect in the dull light afforded by the lurid glare of the burning village. On the night of the 29th the breaching guns were in position, and opened at daybreak on the curtain, which was reported by the townspeople as being the most easily and effectively breached. I say reported, for I believe no plan could be furnished to our engineers, though the fortress was close to one of our largest stations, Mhow.

The guns hurled their 24-pound missiles against the doomed curtain of the fort—the one selected was close to the entrance, which was quite impregnable if guarded by a handful of desperate men, and the approach to it was enfiladed in every direction by musketry and jingals. The first few shots discovered that we had found a tolerably hard nut to crack, the walls were so perfectly and massively built, of a very handsome reddish stone, admirably calculated to resist a pounding. The breaching was continued day and night, for it was now bright moonlight ; and on the 30th the enemy displayed a white flag from the battlements. I think I am wrong, however, in calling it a flag—it was a pair of paijamas. But this answered the purpose. The guns and mortars ceased their growling, and a deputation came outside and were met by another, composed of natives, from us to dictate our terms—"unconditional surrender." However, the mutinous horde did not seem to relish them, and declined to submit to any other than the Rajah of Dhar, ignoring the British rule as a thing that was. This respite cooled the guns, and all commenced a brisker fire than before. Some gunners were badly wounded and killed in the battery, and Lieut. Christie, who had previously had some hair-breadth escapes, was shot through the chest. Our ammunition had been replenished by a new supply from Mhow, brought in by James Rice in a fabulously short time: he was even more eager for rebels than for "particularly fine tigers." Reports now spread about camp that the breach was practicable, and the engineers pronounced it a model path to glory; but to the inexperienced eye it looked a rough and rugged way, so steep, so loose, and dusty, with huge stones and masses of masonry jumbled up together. But the nearer the breach approached completion, the slacker grew the fire from the fort, and it was but too evident the garrison was getting smaller day by day. Yet our Cavalry outposts were more alert than before. Could it be that our shells, which burst so beautifully every two minutes, had decimated the inmates? or was there, as report said, an underground passage to some spot distant from the besieged fortress? That they should have escaped the vigilance of our line of videttes did not enter into the range of possibilities. We began to fear the thirteen lakhs of treasure reported to be inside might find its way out also, and this became a very serious topic, as it had been promised to us as fair prize money, and prize agents for each service were appointed, and the storming party told off, with its reserve. Sunday morning was appointed for the bloody work. On the previous night, however, it was necessary to examine the breach by close inspection, to see that nothing was wanting to ensure success. The Brigadier and staff repaired to the breaching battery for that purpose; the officer commanding the Cavalry said not a mouse could get through his line; two Madras Sapper Sergeants, in disguise, stealthily crossed the deadly four hundred yards over which our shots had sped for days before, and arrived at the foot of the breach in perfect silence. The party near the guns, in breathless curiosity, were watching these two gallant men, who found the breach not only practicable, but the just angle engineers love to make, and on climbing its height found the fort empty! save two or three old and wounded men. This was what fast subalterns termed "a sell." So all the anxious watchers stormed the bloodless breach.

The garrison had not escaped, however, entirely unperceived. Two hours before we gained possession, a sharp firing was heard in the direction of one of the Cavalry outposts. Possibly at this point some few rebels showed themselves, to create a diversion there, whilst the main body trailed out, as only these cowards can, in an entirely opposite direction—it was never clearly settled where, but out they went, nevertheless. Unfortunately, the European Cavalry outposts had been changed that morning, and the men were scarcely acquainted with the ground, and consequently, in galloping towards the spot where the firing was going on, more than half became thoroughly bogged in the marshy ground.

When it was ascertained that the rebels had but just left the fort, the Cavalry were ordered in pursuit, and as they passed *en route* from the camp, the martial strains of the national anthem were heard from the band of the 25th Regiment inside. The pursuit was, however, fruitless. Articles of clothing were scattered along the road, marking their track towards Mundeesoor.

So soon as the capture of the fortress became known in camp, the curious proceeded to make discoveries in it, although it was midnight. The Commissariat officer, two Dragoon officers, and one Medical, while pursuing their investigations by the light afforded from a torch, cleverly inserted it into a heap of loose gunpowder, which blew up their little party, sadly burning one of them, and proved a very wholesome warning to all. Major Robertson, who with his corps was placed in charge of the fort, soon discovered that the treasure was still safe in the palace. The smell everywhere was horrible, proceeding from dead camels, horses, ponies, and men, in all stages of decomposition. Daybreak on the morrow revealed to us the excellent practice our Artillery had made with their shot and shell. The palace was riddled, and a Brahmin, who had been kept a prisoner in the fort during the siege, told us, that so thick and fast did our missiles fall about the treasury, that the rebels dared not venture near it to carry its contents away, as was their intention. They had despoiled the palace of all else; or, more probably, it had been previously emptied by its owner, in readiness for the siege. The interior, when contrasted with the well-built and finished exterior of the place, was disappointing: empty chatties, heaps of grain and salt, charpoys, blood-stained apparel, loose gunpowder, bullets, and sepoys' uniforms, lay scattered about, together with matchlocks, swords, and brass utensils, in great abundance. The guns on the bastions were country-made, and dangerous to work. But the kernel of the nut was contained in large chests in a tiny room, with curiously-painted walls. It consisted of a few jewels, but chiefly of coin—rupees, gold mohurs, and bright yellow Florentine sequins—silver elephant gear, bedsteads, and drinking bowls, amounting to eight or nine lakhs. It was said the wealth was chiefly accumulated by the progenitor of the present Rajah, who was of so miserly a disposition, as to weigh out the grain on which he fed his sacred birds, lest they might get too much. The Dhar jewels were not found. Report said they were hidden in the palace. The Sappers and Miners dug and excavated floors, pulled down walls and closets, but all to no purpose. What treasure we found was placed on seventeen elephants, and sent under a guard into the fort of Mhow, which had undergone enlargement, repair, and a considerable increase in its strength of fortification. A day or two after the capture of Dhar we were reinforced by a large body of Hyderabad Contingent troops of all arms, under command of Major William Orr.

The rebel Commandant in the Fort of Dhar was named Gool Mahomed: he was said to have a wife of more than ordinary beauty with him, and was about to kill her to save her falling into our hands. She very naturally objected to this, but urged him to escape, if possible, and allow her to accompany him, when he could kill her should they be overtaken. The woman's counsel saved them. This is the romance of Dhar: the reality is still to come, the prize money, which the victors await.

CHAPTER III.

THE FORCE MARCHES ON MUNDEESOOR—BATTLE OF MUNDEESOOR—STORMING OF GOOLARIA—RELIEF OF NEEMUCH—FORCE RETURNS TO INDORE—THE RESIDENCY AND CHURCH.

OUR batteries and the fort were dismantled, the wounded were sent to Mhow, and on the 8th of November the force was in motion towards Neemuch. Two days afterwards, at Noyla, we heard the Mehidpoor Contingent had been defeated by the rebels, and some of the Officers and European Sergeants killed. Major Timmins, the Commandant, and Lieutenant Dysart, the Adjutant, escaped, and arrived in our Camp: the latter officer, with a handful of faithful men, fought their guns to the last, and killed some forty of the rebels before yielding. The main body of the Contingent joined the rebels at once, and marched away with the guns and ammunition in great quantity, twenty-six hackery loads in all. They were not, however, to escape unmolested. The Hyderabad Contingent troops, under Major Orr, were sent to cut them off from Mundeesoor. They overtook them as they were passing a river close to Cassegaum, and cut up three or four hundred, taking ninety-four prisoners, and a number of guns with ammunition. In this gallant affair the Contingent Cavalry suffered severely, the Staff officer was very dangerously wounded, and Capts. Clarke and Murray had their chargers shot under them.

The heavy guns of our Force proved a sad hindrance to anything like long marches, so they were left behind, under a guard, to come on at their fastest pace. It was necessary our movements should be accelerated, for report said the Fort of Neemuch was besieged, and all communication with it cut off. On the 18th we reached the Chumbul river, which delayed us a day crossing. A drumhead court martial assembled on the Mehidpoor prisoners at five P. M., a parade was ordered, and seventy-four villainous-looking fellows shot

On the morning of the 21st we arrived before

Mundeesoor, and a reconnoitring party ascended a hill in our front which hid the city from us. The enemy made a show in considerable force, but we were not to attack them that day. The Brigade encamped, leaving a strong force on the heights, in command of Major Robertson. It was a mile distant from our Camp, and the city much further. The enemy, perhaps construing our inactivity into fear, were not to be disappointed of the day's fighting they had made up their minds to have, so they came out in great numbers, crossing a river in their passage, and attacked Major Robertson's Force. He opened the guns on them, and directed Lieutenant Dew, of H. M.'s 14th Dragoons, and Captain Orr, of the Nizam's Cavalry, to charge. They did so most gallantly: the former officer, with but twenty men, dashed into a mass of about 300 footmen, for which act of valour he was unsuccessfully recommended for that most prized of all decorations, the Victoria Cross. The enemy apparently had little calculated on such resistance from so small a force, and made a most precipitate retreat to the river, being pursued to its brink, and many being shot in crossing. Thus, before the Brigade and Staff could arrive to take part in the affair, the enemy had been driven back, with the loss of one hundred killed and numbers wounded.

On the following morning at dawn we marched, most of us supposing, to take Mundeesoor. The Cavalry and Artillery advanced, and drew a few shots from the guns in the town, which being large, straggling, and full of trees, hid the enemy from us. Their pickets fell in as we advanced, with the whole of our baggage and followers, and skirted round the town until we had gained the Neemuch road. As this required some caution it was not accomplished until mid-day, when we halted in jowarree fields. Here some twenty or more inhabitants came out in great fear. They told us the main body of the rebels had left, but that two thousand still remained in the Fort. It soon became evident, however, that this enemy was to remain in our rear, and we commenced crossing the river to encamp. While so doing, intelligence was received of a body of this enemy in great force coming towards Mundeesoor. The Cavalry dashed through the river, and advanced to meet them at a smashing pace, across country, through fields of standing grain: it was not until after some five miles' gallop that the enemy came in sight, when they were seen making rapidly for the cover of a village, which those mounted managed to reach. The Fourteenth and Nizam's Cavalry got amongst their infantry, and accounted for upwards of a hundred, chasing them within matchlock range of the mud walls of the village, where the enemy was assembled in considerable strength, and, seeing we were without Infantry or guns, taunted, and endeavoured to draw us on. As it was getting dark, dismounting Cavalry to storm was not advisable. Moreover, they were in very superior numbers, two Officers and some Troopers on our side had been wounded, men and horses were fatigued and without rations, and we marched to rejoin the Force again, killing numbers of men on our return, who had been hidden in trees and standing corn.

On the morrow the Force again attempted to cross the river, but, as the baggage was being transported, some alarm was visible among the followers. As the garrison had sallied out of the Fort, and appeared to be advancing, a Troop of Dragoons re-crossed, and proved a warning to them to remain where they were. At length the *impedimenta* were on the opposite side of the river, and with a strong advanced guard the Force marched for Neemuch, distant twenty-two miles, when simultaneously with the report of cannon in front was a cry that the rear guard was assailed, and on a hill to our right a large body of the enemy were descried. The alarm among the followers grew quite amusing, and bullock hackeries that had never advanced beyond a snail's pace before, were seen performing chariot races now, the women and children adding to the din.

A Troop of the 14th Dragoons, with Lieutenants Leith, Redmayne, and Chapman, went to the rear guard, which had not been engaged, but was threatened. This reinforcement kept the rebels at bay for a time. The guns of our Brigade now opened on the enemy, who had appeared in front, his right resting beyond the village of Goolaria, and his left on a ridge eastward of that place; while his Battery of six guns were placed on his right centre, and masked by date, palm and other trees. Behind their guns were some ruined houses, which sheltered the Infantry and some Mehidpoor Contingent Cavalry, and on the left of their Battery was a deep cutting, or gharry-road. Our Force formed up, and Woolcombe's. Hungerford's battery opened at nine hundred yards, and after a few rounds Captain Hungerford made a brilliant movement to the right front, and enfiladed the enemy's line; and, following up his advantage, he and Lieutenant Martin, with his support of thirty of the Fourteenth Dragoons, charged across the cutting into the enemy's guns, taking them; but so hot was the musketry fire from the huts that they were oblige to retire. Lieutenant Martin was severely wounded. Our line of Infantry, the 25th, and H. M.'s 86th Regiment on its right, had, by a well-directed fire, previously cleared the guns to a considerable extent, while Major Orr's force of Hyderabad Troops deployed on our left to support the general attack, and his Cavalry hovered on our flanks. So soon as Captain Hungerford and the Dragoons retired from the battery, Captain Gall led his reserve squadron to the front, and charged, capturing the six guns, and cutting down the gunners. Just at this crisis the rear guard was hard pressed, the enemy being but eight hundred yards distant from Lieutenant Fenwick, commanding it. The whole of the Nizam's Cavalry, commanded by Captains Abbott and Murray, with two guns and three companies of Infantry, was sent to reinforce it, as the main body of the enemy from our front had been driven into the village of Goolaria, which they reached without much loss. The Cavalry proceeded to scour the country around the village, and met large bodies of men laden with all kinds of plunder ; so that it became at once evident these were the Neemuch rebels. We discovered afterwards, that, having received intelligence of our approach, they raised the siege they had laid to the Neemuch garrison, and were endeavouring to reach Mundeesoor, when we so opportunely met them. Hundreds were cut up by the Nizam's Cavalry, led by Captain Orr, on the left side of the village, and the Dragoons, by Captain Gall, on the right. The variety of loot being brought from Neemuch is beyond description—carriages, horses, household furniture of all kinds, carpets, crockery, glass, military drums, instruments musical and surgical, fishing tackle, books, clothing, &c. It was a rich harvest for the camp-followers. While the country was being cleared by the cavalry, the infantry and guns had drawn up before the village of Goolaria, which, being mud-built, was but little affected by round shot or shell. The infantry found many rebels hidden in hay stacks, which were fired. Some perished thus, others, when on fire, ran for the village, but fell victims to the Enfields of the 86th.

When the reinforcements reached the rear, they discovered that the Mundeesoor garrison, numbering about two thousand men, had made a descent on our baggage. The two guns opened on them, and drove them back, and the two Regiments of Nizam's Cavalry, and a troop of the 14th Dragoons, led by Lieutenant Leith, charged the retiring masses of Infantry, killing many, and pursuing them up to a point where a small pond of water and some shallow pits or stone quarries joined. The enemy advanced beyond these, endeavouring to draw the cavalry into the broken ground. Lieutenant Redmayne, who was leading, wheeled round the pond, being closely followed by Lieutenant Chapman and a few dragoons. A tremendous volley from the gravel quarries, and Lieutenant Redmayne died a soldier's death, but was mercilessly cut up by the rebels, who carried off his charger and accoutrements. The former was subsequently recovered by Sir Hugh Rose at the capture of Fort Ratghur. Most of the men, who had closely followed Lieutenant Redmayne, were more or less wounded. At this juncture, Captain Abbott arrived by a different route on the other side of the water and gravel pits, and the enemy retreated into the Mundeesoor fort. As night was closing on us, we gave the rebels the time of darkness for repose in Goolaria, our cavalry surrounding the village. The remainder of the Brigade encamped, but was disturbed soon after by a false alarm. The cold was intense, and as the cavalry pickets and outposts could not light fires, it was much felt; and the enemy even in the dark kept up a matchlock fire. While we were crouching beside our horses in the darkness, one of the dragoons fancied he saw a figure crawling between the videttes so as to make his escape. The dragoon fastened his horse, and, unperceived, stole after the retiring object. He found it to be one of the rebels, from whose hand he snatched a sword, and slew him.

On the following morning, the 24th, the whole Force, save a guard for the camp, which was left standing, proceeded to storm the village in which the enemy were. After a shower of shot and shell to clear the walls and houses of their sharp shooters, the Royal County Downs, the 25th Regiment, Nizam's Infantry, and Madras Sappers and Miners, led by Majors Keane, Robertson, and officers commanding the two remaining corps, rushed across the range under fire, over the mud walls, and amid the burning houses began to shoot and bayonet the mutineers, who had themselves fired some of the houses, to make the smoke and confusion the greater. The defenders had got up in the roofs of the houses, and poured a deadly matchlock fire from the eaves into our red coats, as they dashed along the streets. The Madrassees, with their huge blue turbans, behaved gloriously, as they always do. They were rushing about like salamanders in the flames and smoke. From midday until evening the bloody work went on, the County Downs despising all means but the bayonet. Occasionally a son of the sister isle, all covered with sweat and dust, his face blackened by powder and smoke, would be seen leading tenderly outside the walls a woman or child; and a cavalry Assistant Surgeon humanely carried to a place of safety a Rajpoot girl whose leg had been smashed by a carbine shot. She was of good family, and had lost a father and brother in the fray. All the rebels who ventured to rush from the burning village were sabred by the cavalry. Hand-to-hand fights were going on in the patches of sugar-cane near the village, and about two hundred Velliattees came out *en masse* under a flag of truce, surrendering as prisoners. At evening some few only remained, in strongly-built houses at the upper end of the village. Captain Robertson was taking a nine-pounder in to blow open the doors, as the infantry bugles rang out the assembly, and a more thirsty and powder-besmeared body of soldiers could not exist than came forth after the day's work. Cavalry pickets were again thrown out around the ruins in which this handful of desperate men remained, and the Brigade encamped. The next day not a living soul remained in Goolaria. Neemuch was now most successfully relieved, and Captain Mayne, with an escort of sowars, rode in, and returned, accompanied by some of the besieged officers. In due time after these events the Despatches appeared, and of course "where all behaved so well it were invidious, &c." The heads of Departments were mentioned and thanked, and Lieut. Martin's gallantry was noticed—and he well deserved it. Brigadier Stuart was made a Companion of the Bath, and Colonel Durand, with Captains Gall, Robertson, Woolcombe, and Hungerford, received a step in rank for their services.

The Neemuch garrison had been besieged for many days, and on one occasion scaling ladders were placed against the walls, and the rebels, with their fanatical cry, proceeded to mount them, soon, however, taking to their heels, leaving their ladders behind. One was evidently constructed on a new principle, for the occasion, being mounted on four wheels. On another occasion a fakeer, with a mirror fixed on his breast, walked round the fort under fire, having stated that if he succeeded in completing the circle round the walls, the place would fall into their hands. At first, and for great part of the distance round, the bullets flew harmlessly past him: at length one brought him down. A bandsman went out, and brought his head and the mirror into the fort, and disabused the sepoys, who had grown somewhat superstitious, of his supposed magical powers. But where British officers worked as gunners, and ladies made up ammunition, there was little to be feared so long as provisions lasted. The Bombay 2nd Cavalry, with some Artillery, occasionally made sallies out against bodies of the enemy, and on several occasions had officers killed and wounded. It was in this way the gallant Captain Tucker met his death. The rebels carried his head in triumph to the city of Mundeesoor, and placed it over the gateway of the city. It was found when our Force returned thither, though they had removed it from that position, and it was buried. The heads of two rebel chieftains occupied the vacancy over the gate when we left the city. Grim and hideous they looked, and read a most wholesome moral to the budmashes, of whom the city was full. Numbers had hidden, but were taken prisoners. At length a small body of Europeans was sent in to search : some of these were wounded as they entered dark rooms to bring out ruffians who had concealed themselves there. The two thousand which garrisoned the fort had gone off on the evening of their defeat, with all their loot, to Naghur, but they broke up their standards, saying their gods had forsaken them.

Colonel Durand, the Governor General's Agent, now directed the Force to march back on Indore ; Captain Macdonald, the Quarter

Master General of the Force, left to join Sir Hugh Rose; and some faithful Sikhs of the Bhopal Contingent were placed under the command of Captain H. O. Mayne, and formed the nucleus of "Mayne's Horse," now stationed at Goonah; and we relinquished our old name of the "Malwa" for that of the "Nerbudda Field Force."

En route to Indore we passed through Mehidpoor, on the banks of the Sipra River. It had been a model cantonment before the mutiny, but now presented all the signs of the recent disturbances there—blackened walls of houses, with quantities of furniture in them undestroyed, gardens, flourishing as though nothing had blighted the place. The parade ground, on which Dysart fought to the last for his guns, was still strewn with caps, arms, epaulettes, and ammunition. One big gun, too, remained, which was too cumbrous for the rebels to move. The trees were torn to pieces by the grape and canister, and a row of nineteen graves lay beneath them. In each were four or five men their comrades had buried, and two other bodies were hung up before we left.

On the 10th of December we passed the spot

from whence Sir Thomas Hyslop first saw the enemy when he won the battle of Mehidpoor, and struck a final blow at the house of Holkar.

On the 11th we arrived at Oojein, and were saluted by the guns of the Begum; and on the 15th we reached Indore, which was understood by all in the force to be a hot-bed of mutineers, and Colonel Durand was bent on bringing them to account. Indeed, it was not certain that Holkar's troops would not oppose our entry; and Holkar himself was reported to be gone on a shooting expedition. But our entry was peaceful. It was reported that twelve hundred cavalry had given up their arms, and some newly-raised Mahrattas had charge of his artillery, but some regiments of infantry had still to be dealt with. The force encamped in the Residency gardens and grounds, the buildings of which were all unroofed by fire, and the solid masonry of the Residency bore the marks of round shot. The remnants of the once elegant furniture, which had been re-collected by the Maharaja, lay in strata of motley composition on the ground floor. The Church was desecrated—the windows gone, the bell torn down, the whole interior furniture gone, save the altar rail, over which some European soldier had written a verse, not inappropriate, from the 19th chapter of the 1st Book of Kings—" *They have forsaken thy covenant, thrown down thine altars, and slain thy prophets with the sword; and I, even I only, am left; and they seek my life, to take it away.*" The Europeans who were murdered here, were buried in the cemetery by order of Holkar, and the Force naturally expected a heavy retribution would be made. But Sir Robert Hamilton's advent was announced, and Colonel Durand, who united the talent of an engineer with his political position, departed, very much regretted by all.

CHAPTER IV.

SIR HUGH ROSE ASSUMES COMMAND OF THE FORCE, NOW CONSISTING OF TWO BRIGADES—SECOND BRIGADE AT SEHORE—PUNISHMENT OF THE MUTINEERS OF THE BHOPAL CONTINGENT—SIEGE AND REDUCTION OF RATGHUR—ACTION AT BORODIA—RELIEF OF SAUGOR—CAPTURE OF GARRAKOTTA—ACTION IN THE PASS OF MUDDENPORE.

AT this time, a new era dawned on our force. A general who shed the brightest lustre on our arms joined us—a man who went from victory to victory. Though he knew nothing of India and its customs, and less of its languages, he took and kept his own counsel, set at nought routine and red-tapism, while inculcating the most rigid discipline. His tactics and strategy were entirely new, and astonished those whose beards had grown grey in the service. He won his battles with the most unparallelled dash and intrepidity —no stronghold could hold out against such determination. See how Gwalior fell, and contrast it with the tardiness we read of across the Jumna. There were not wanting those who thought and said his tactics were incorrect. Infantry men did not relish battles being won by cavalry and artillery, almost ere the line of combatants was formed. He was no common man of the old school, but a genius born for that and greater occasions still. This man is Sir Hugh Rose. And though never once praised by him, I feel—as all who served under him must do—proud and glad that it was reserved to me to serve throughout the campaign in Central India. The world knows his fame and his reward. His health was injured, and the interest of his exploits began to wane ere his despatches appeared, and much was lost to him. What was suffered from the burning sun and scourching thirst by hundreds of his men, can never be told. Their eyes are closed in death, their bones bleach on the plains of Hindostan. The survivors' reward is told in six months' batta, and a clasp shared in common with two other Forces. That we expected a special mark, I need not write here.

Sir Hugh Rose having assumed command, the force marched into Mhow, and remained there until the 30th of December. All haste was made to complete the siege train, and improve the carriage of the Force, so as to render it as little as possible a hackery campaign. Malwa and Rajpootana yielded thousands of camels, but these were insufficient. The camel ambulances for the sick were of an admirable description. Officers were compelled to leave their heavy baggage behind. Thus equipped, the force was once more transported to Indore, and at 2 A. M. the next morning was suddenly turned out to invest the city, which was surrounded until the evening ; while the Major-General, with a small body of men, assembled the whole of the soldiers of the Maharajah in a plain near camp, he himself seeing them all out of their lines. They mustered hundreds strong What became of them we knew not : evidence against them must have been wanting. Holkar had promised to deliver up the ringleaders of the mutiny, but scarcely a score were brought to the front. Some few were hanged, and one or two blown away from guns. The blood of the murdered was yet fresh about the jail, and a woman's scalp, with long fair hair, was found in the fields.

On the 8th of January, the Major-General left our camp with a troop of Dragoons and some Hyderabad Contingent artillery, and proceeded to Sehore to join the 2nd Brigade, under Colonel Stuart, H.' M.'s 14th Light Dragoons, which had arrived there from the Dekkan by a different route. At this station near one hundred and fifty mutineers of the Bhopal Contingent, which had in great part proved faithless, were put to a merciful death. Anticipating what was in store for them, they made a futile attempt to escape, and, consequently, many brought their career to a close a few hours sooner. They were killed by the sentries and guards placed over them.

Sir Hugh Rose now pushed on with all haste, with the 2nd Brigade C. I. F. F., and Hyderabad Contingent Force, for the purpose of relieving Saugor, the last and then only remaining besieged garrison. Here, and shut within the narrow walls of the Fort, were three hundred and seventy-one souls, many being helpless women and children, all without the necessaries of life. Disease was rife among them, and had carried off twenty-two, while the population around was thirsting for the blood of the remainder. But ere these could be set at liberty, the stronghold of Ratghur had to be reduced, and blood-guilty chieftains punished. With this work in view, and the depths of every national feeling stirred in the breasts of the European element of the Force, it marched from Bagrode to Ratghur on the 24th of January. At 5 P. M. the enemy were seen in position lining the banks of the Beena river, a stream running on the west side of the Fort. The Cavalry and Horse Artillery crossed, and drove the rebels into the shelter of the town and Fort. It being then nightfall, the Brigade encamped. The enemy killed one dragoon, and one native officer of the 24th Native Infantry, and seriously wounded Apothecary Conway.

On the following day the Major-General and Divisional Staff, with a Cavalry escort, made a reconnoissance, and did not reach his tent until 5-30 P. M., having been absent the entire day, thus beginning the campaign with an energy and recklessness of exposure which he sustained up to his departure from the Force at Gwalior. Ratghur fort is situated on a hill of pyriform shape, of considerable extent, and, as is the case with all the fortresses in Bundelcund, buried in jungle. The fortifications were built on the large extremity of the hill, which was precipitous on all sides save one spot, which was narrow and steep. This was the spot selected by Major Boileau, Madras Engineers, for the breaching operation, and at night the entire hill was invested by the Brigade and native Troops of H. H. the Begum of Bhopal.

On the 26th, part of the Force drew the attention of the garrison away to the end of the fort, near the town, whilst the General and Staff, with the 3rd European Regiment, took possession of the vulnerable path, and placed the heavy guns there. These at once began to inflict heavy blows on the double enceinte of the walls, and the Madras Sappers threw up a mortar battery to keep down the enemy's fire, which began to get warm on this point. During these operations the remainder of the force took possession of the town, and Lightfoot's Battery occupied the Eedgha, from which point also the fort was shelled, and several prisoners were taken in the town. The garrison was said to number five or six hundred men, Velaities, Mekranics, and Bundeelas, rudely skilled in war, but fighting men from their boyhood. Just as the breach began to become practicable, a futile attempt was made by 2000 allies of the same description to relieve the garrison. Our Cavalry outposts and videttes engaged them, but from the wooded nature of the ground, and difficult bed of the Beena river, their action was much paralysed. They were obliged to fight singly and in small detachments, a style of fighting to which regular Cavalry are not used. The Artillery, together with Hyderabad Infantry under Captain Hare, and some troopers under Lieut. Westmacott, joined in the attack, and drove them through the river, and the Major-General pursued them to Chunderapoor.

That night, as in the Fort of Dhar the night previous to the storm, an ominous stillness reigned, and one attempt to escape from the main gate had been detected by the 3rd Europeans. This was probably a feint, whilst the mass of the enemy stole out at a sallyport and lowered themselves by ropes, subsequently passing through the tract invested by the Bhopal troops. Lieutenant Strutt of the Artillery discovered the empty state of the fort, and with some soldiers of the 3rd European Regt. walked through the breach. In it were a few animals, and amongst them the charger which Lieutenant Redmayne lost when he fell at Mundeesoor. It had received a severe shell-wound over the eye, and was bought by Sir Hugh Rose. The Shazadah of Mundeesoor, in whose possession it was after the battle at that place, had brought it here, and abandoned it when he fled. There was grain and water in the fort, but no treasure. The escape of the rebels here was nothing like so complete as at Dhar. The Cavalry gave pursuit, about seventy were cut up, and several of the rebel chieftains, and nearly one hundred of their followers, fell into our hands as prisoners. Among the former was Mahomed Fazil Khan, who was discovered hiding, having been unable to get through our videttes. A mehta in Captain Need's service was the fortunate individual who found him, and received the thousand rupees which had been set on his head by Government. At night his carcase hung over the gate of the fort, side by side with Kamdar Khan, who had received a jagheer in Kolara from the Government at the close of the Pindarree war. The old hatred for the English and their adherents had in no way been appeased by the grant of land, for at the first outbreak of the mutiny he raised his standard and marched with his followers on Barsiah, burning the Government bungalow there, and massacreing two Hindoos and one Musalman in political employ. The admirable way in which the prisoners here were dealt with, did much to tranquillise this part of India, and saved much future bloodshed. The standards taken here, as at Mundeesoor, were marked with the crescent and "bloody hand."

On the 31st, Sir Hugh Rose left Ratghur with a Battery and Troop of Artillery, three troops of the Fourteenth and two of Bombay Dragoons, together with some mortars, European and Native Infantry, and the Madras Sappers and Miners. He led this force through twelve miles of dense jungle, which required the greatest precaution, the enemy being ready to cut off anything straggling or in the rear. As soon as we approached the village of Borodia they opened a brisk musketry fire.

They were in dense jungle on the bank of a river, and, after the loss of some horses on our side, they were driven through the river by the skirmishers of the 3rd European Regiment, and Captain, now Major, Forbes, C.B., with part of his Regiment, made a dashing charge across it, cutting up a number as they were retiring on their position in the village and surrounding jungle. The enemy, adopting French tactics on the occasion, placed his guns in the village, and—with better success than usually attends such position for Artillery—got them out again when he abandoned it. Our Artillery, having crossed the river, opened fire on Borodia, which fire for a short time was well returned, and cost us some casualties; amongst others, Captain Neville of the Engineers, who had just joined the Divisional Staff. As the day began to close, Colonel Liddle led the Infantry on to assault the village, while Lieutenant Strutt shelled the fort; but the rebels fled through the jungle in the rear, having suffered considerable loss, and the capture of men of note among them. From the wooded nature of the ground, which hid the disposition of our enemy, the day's combat was not without considerable loss on our side also. Fatigued by the day's exertions, we marched back to our camp at Ratghur the same night. Some rain fell at this time, and the nights were very cold, contrasted with the hot sun in the day, time. Pittman, of the Bombay Horse Artillery, had a narrow escape during the action—a round-shot grazed and severely hurt his shoulder.

After these two signal defeats, the rebels retired beyond Jilla to Korye, and two other strongholds, Muriaoli and Bhopyle, from which they threatened Saugor, were evacuated. The fortifications and defences at Ratghur were laid waste by the Engineers, and Sir Hugh Rose led his force in triumph into Saugor. The most unqualified demonstrations of joy greeted him from the inmates of the Fort, who were then in their seventh month of confinement. Thanks to some small accident connected with a dispute over some treasure, a part of the Bengal sepoys stationed at Saugor had not joined in the mutiny, and the houses and property in the Cantonments were intact. Shouts of welcome, and an enthusiastic display of handkerchiefs from the ladies of the garrison, greeted the arrival of the troops, and in a few hours all the sufferings undergone were forgotten, and the Force passed some days in revelry and rejoicing. But in the mean time the lead was taken from the grooves of the Enfield rifles, the tumbrils and waggons were filled, a large bazaar was organized, and the road to Mhow and Bombay was opened for reinforcements and supplies. Lieutenant Prendergast, of the Madras Engineers, with a party of Sappers and Miners, was engaged destroying the rebel defences of Nowrowlee, twelve miles distant, and Captain Hare, of the Hyderabad Contingent, with Troops of that service, marched on the fort of Tanoda, with a view to its reduction, while the Major General prepared to march to the fort of Garrakotah.

Early in February, the 2nd Brigade C. I. F. F. marched from Saugor, leaving a troop of H. M.'s 14th Light Dragoons, and two companies of the 24th B. N. I., to protect the station. In two marches it reached Bussarree, near Garrakotah, and encamped there: the latter place was in the hands of the enemy. Two small rivulets, branches of the Sonar river, run near it strengthening, it as a position, the water almost coming up to the fort walls, serving as a moat to it, and where water was absent dense jungle supplied its place: it was a spot well suited to its occupants, and was built with great solidity. Captain Hare rejoined the Force here, the rebels having evacuated Sonoda, leaving their supplies and stores.

On the evening of our arrival, Lieutenant Dick, with the 3rd Light Cavalry, had an affair with a party of rebels on picket duty, and killed a few of them. The Garrison disputed our possession of the village near the fort, and endeavoured to keep us out of it. The Bombay Horse and Foot Batteries opened on them, and the 3rd European Regiment carried the place by assault, but the mutineers continued to annoy them the night through, making futile attempts to drive them out again.

On the following day, after some skirmishing, our guns and mortars were pushed still nearer the fort, and Sir Hugh Rose and his Staff, according to his custom, proceeded to reconnoitre and invest it as far as practicable. The Garrison, however, did not wait for the cord to be drawn round them, but escaped by the Paunch Ghat towards Dumoh. Captain Hare, in command of a Troop of sowars and two Horse Artillery guns, together with Captain Need and his Troop of the 14th Light Dragoons, started at once in pursuit, and came up with them on the river Boes, a tributary of the Sonar. Captain Need led the Cavalry across it, and was in the midst of the rebels instanter. Here, as in so many subsequent actions, he distinguished himself by his bravery and swordmanship: the Cavalry slew a hundred men, and of these Captain Need killed five.

At this time (11th February) the 1st Brigade was at Tonk, marching on Chanderi, Major Boileau and the Madras Sappers and Miners commenced the destruction of the fort of Garrakottah, and the Major General and Force returned to Saugor, where he was detained organising the Commissariat Department until the end of the month, at which time he again set out to join the 1st Brigade, and wrest Jhansi from the hands of the mutineers.

We reached Raghvas on the 1st of March (it is distant 26 miles N. E. of Saugor), and effected a junction with the Hyderabad Contingent Force under Major Orr, who had preceded us to gain information of the rebel movements, and also to reconnoitre the country: they had collected in considerable force about the hilly districts of Shahghur, Marowra, and Multowa, places which became ultimately familiar to those who shared in the pursuit of Tantia Topee. A range of wooded hills separates the district of Saugor from that of Tihree, and is passable to a force but at three points, and it was at these we encountered opposition: they were all naturally difficult, and had been strengthened by all the rude appliances the rebels could devise. Sir Hugh Rose determined to force the Pass of Muddenpore, while Major Scudamore of the 14th Dragoons made a feigned attempt to pass the range at their strongest position, Narrat. Consequently, on our first arrival before the passes, the Major-General sent out a party of Cavalry to reconnoitre a small fort about three miles from our camp (it was situated on a hill side, and near a village): this party was fired on, and returned. In the afternoon, Major Scudamore's force, consisting of some 3rd Europeans, Dragoons, Irregulars, and a mortar, marched on the village in question. A brisk fire was opened on them and returned, lasting for two hours, after which Captain Macdonald, with three companies of his Regiment (the 3rd Europeans) carried the village by force of the bayonet: fifty of the enemy were killed, and fifty-two taken prisoners; the remainder escaped from the west side of the fort, and retired into the jungles beyond. Sir Hugh Rose, with a strong advance guard, arrived at the pass of Muddenpore, and was at once under the fire of its defenders, supposed to number nine thousand men, chiefly Bundeelas and Velliatees, with a few Bengal Sepoys. They were on the left side of the gorge, which was rocky and precipitous, and covered by shrubs. Major Orr's Artillery opened fire on them, but he was obliged to withdraw his guns from the deadly aim of the concealed sharp-shooters. The Hyderabad and 3rd European Infantry skirmished along the hill side, and dislodged them. Some native police joined in the work, and drove the rebels beyond the glen, when they retreated into another hill, where the Bombay Artillery shelled them, and Captain Macdonald with the Grenadiers, and Nos. 1, 2, and 3 companies of the 3rd Regiment, charged them under a heavy fire, inflicting on them a most decisive loss. The remainder of that Regiment, with the Nizam's Infantry, now cleared the whole of the hills, and Captain Abbott, with Irregular Horse, drove the rebels to the village of Muddenpore, where they had a battery of six guns. A few rounds from our guns caused them to retreat again through the jungle to a fort called Sooree, where Captain Abbott still followed them, cutting up a few. At night they evacuated this place also, leaving us their guns, grain, tentage, cattle, and ammunition: from thence they probably retreated to Shahghur, the Rajah of which place commanded them, while the Rajah of Banpoor commanded at the Pass of Narrat.

Having now forced our way through the barrier of the Tihree country, we marched several miles forward, and encamped in open ground, and halted until the 5th, when we reached the fort of Morowzo, a strong position, and a large town partly surrounded by water: this too we found evacuated; the Union Jack was hoisted on the heights at sunrise, a salute of twenty-one guns was fired, and it became a British possession. A large party of Cavalry and Infantry was sent forth to seek the Rajah, supposed to have secreted himself in a village ten miles distant, but he was not found. The loss to the enemy while forcing the pass was estimated at three hundred men. The remainder now left the Shahghur country and marched on Tolbrit, near Jhansi, and our Force followed them ; but this beautiful fortress was in turn abandoned as as we approached, and without further hostilities the 2nd Brigade appeared before Jhansi.

CHAPTER V.

FIRST BRIGADE MARCHES ON CHANDERI—ATTACK ON THE OUTPOST AT FUTTYABAD—SKIRMISH AT THE KATTEE GATTEE—SIEGE, STORM, AND CAPTURE OF CHANDERI.

THE 1st Brigade was detained in Mhow until the arrived of the 21st Co. Royal Engineers, a Royal battery, and six hundred more of H. M.'s 86th Regt., and did not march until the 6th of February. As it passed through Malwa the heat had already become great in the day-time, and the hemp and poppy fields were in full bloom. While at Dacocha Mr. Layard passed through our camp, travelling post in a shigram, in which he appears to have gained his experience of the country. At Dewass our siege train, some miles in length when moving, joined us. We kept the line of the Agra Trunk road as far as Goonah. The telegraph posts and wire had almost disappeared, all the dak bungalows were burnt, and the Mussulman tombs and temples were being regenerated. From Goonah we marched into Bundlekund, in the direction of Easaughur, in the territory of Scindia. Here it was reported the rebels had mustered very strong, and were manufacturing both gunpowder and guns in the fort, and determined to oppose our passage of the river near the town. The Brigadier therefore altered the line of march, and proceeded towards Chanderi, in latitude 24° 41′, longitude 78° 12′, south of Agra 170 miles. On arriving at Koorsara, a small village six miles short of Chanderi, the force encamped, and a reconnoitring party of Dragoons and Irregular Horse, accompanied by Captain Gall, Fenwick, R. E., Keatinge, Political Agent, and Assistant Surgeon Sylvester, proceeded through the dense jungle in the direction of that place. Columns of smoke, however, towered in the air about every half mile. These proceeded from fires lit by the concealed enemy as we approached them, and a regular line of these columns appeared extending to Chanderi fort itself, warning the garrison of our approach. At length we reached a gorge in sandstone hills, covered with trees and underwood, and were about to emerge from it, having caught a glimpse of the distant fort, and a temple which stood still nearer, when we were received with a volley of musketry. It would have been folly to have gone further without infantry to clear the jungle. We had ascertained the enemy was there, and returned to camp.

Next day, with a strong advanced guard under Major Robertson, we advanced on this once-important place, formerly containing fourteen thousand stone houses, three hundred and eighty-four markets, three hundred aud sixty caravanseras, and twelve thousand mosques. Mahratta oppression has brought it to its present state, which is one of most picturesque and beautiful architectural ruin. Our advanced guard had reached the gorge just mentioned, when the enemy opened a brisk fire on it. The infantry, in skirmishing order, ascended either side of the defile, covering the hill sides to their summits. The red coats dotted among the green foliage rendered it far more picturesque than martial. Arrived at the level ground beyond, we saw great numbers of the enemy in the ruined temple and summer houses in our front. The Artillery opened with round shot and shell, driving the mutineers into another tract of jungle beyond, from which again they were driven still nearer the fort, and took shelter behind a wall of recent construction, which extended from one ridge of hills to another opposite, the valley intervening. The wall was loopholed, and furnished with bastions twelve or fourteen feet in height and several in thickness. It was a grand position, and ought to have held out against us for some time, especially as our field pieces made no impression on the masonry, and it completely held us from any advance on the fort and town in that direction. But the Infantry rushed on with an impetuosity not easily checked, and gained the wall in a moment. The enemy retreated to the town and fort, about half a mile distant. The wall was destroyed, a force was left at the spot, and the brigade skirted round one of the ranges of hills which commanded the fort, and encamped.

We were not molested, and on the morrow (7th of March) proceeded to clear the ridge in question, which, like the whole country surrounding, was wooded. It was of sandstone, and a hundred feet in height, with a passage cut through the solid rock, called the "Kattee Gattee." The fort was visible to us through this extraordinary tunnel, over which was an inscription stating that Ghiasuddin, King of Delhi, caused to be made the lofty gate of Goomtee and Kerolie, near one of the many beautiful tanks near the town. We killed a few of the enemy here, and at the small village of Ramnuggur, at the foot of the hill. The Brigadier and Staff gained the heights: from them a panoramic view of the country beneath was visible, and the fort, which is of about the same height, and built an on isolated hill, was only separated by a wide jungly ravine, about as broad as the range of a nine-pounder. At first sight it looked almost impregnable, but at one spot a ridge of rock ran across the valley, forming a sort of road. Across this was evidently the vulnerable part, but the fortifications had been strengthened at the spot where the ridge joined the fort hill, by means of two towers and a bastion of solid masonry. This curtain was chosen for breaching. Forty years ago it had been taken by blockade by Baptiste, a General of Scindiah's, and during the independence of Malwa it was besieged by Mahmood

Khillji, and surrendered after a siege of eight months. Rana Sanka, the formidable Rajpoot adversary of Baber, had wrested Chanderi from Ibrahim, the sovereign of Delhi, in 1526, and gave it in feudal grant to one of his followers. "Baber in 1528, coveting the place, vowed to wage feudal war against it, and, entering it by escalade, the Rajpoots, after performing their fearful rite of juhar by the massacre of their women and children, rushed, naked and desperate, on the Mussulmans, until they were slain to a man." Such is a brief history of this very formidable fortress, the land belonging to which helped to maintain the late Gwalior Contingent.

The remains of Baptiste's old road for guns up the ridge still were visible, and with great labour some field guns and mortars were got up, and opened fire on the palace, which was a prominent feature. But the enemy's guns replied well, and with good practice; neither could they be silenced. It now became necessary to make a road along the crest of the ridge, in order to get our heavy guns in position to breach. The men were very much exposed to the enemy's fire, there being no other protection than trees; so that much night-work was necessitated. This occupied many days, and on the 10th the Artillery and Engineers, by aid of elephants, dragged up the 24-pounders, and the Cavalry reconnoitred daily; but it was not a country for horsemen to act. The wall and temple we had taken from the enemy on our first arrival had been given into the keeping of some of Scindiah's troops (the place was called Futtyabad), and on the night of the 10th the enemy made a sally out and recaptured the wall.

The 25th Regiment was sent down to repossess themselves of it, and hold it, which they did. The breaching commenced, the range being a very short one and point blank. As the battery was slightly over the eminence, any one, to approach it, had to run the gauntlet of the enemy's fire.

'Twas evident Chanderi had not been so disturbed for many a year. Most of the trees were of a flowering description, and covered with gorgeous blossoms; while flights of parrots screamed among them, monkeys chattered at the soldiery, an occasional panther was turned out of his lair, and wild ducks wheeled overhead. But the sun was fierce and hot, and it was a very thirsty tour of duty in all the batteries, which were five in number. The breaching battery being nearest the fort, was the object of the enemy's special attention, and they kept up an incessant fire on it, both from their cannon and small arms. One individual, who possessed a European rifle, and had learnt to use it, caused much annoyance and many wounds, and the bullocks bringing up ammunition afforded them excellent marks. They appeared to have an unlimited number of guns and wall pieces, extending completely round the fortifications. Our shells fell thick and fast into the fort, and did them much damage ; but as it was so large, they had plenty of space and shelter to escape from them, and an underground passage down the rock into the town close beneath, whereby they got both provisions and water, and occasionally stole the baggage animals which had left camp to graze ; on one occasion killed some camp-followers when foraging ; and on the night of the 13th they ascended a hill overlooking our camp and fired a regular volley into it, but did us no damage.

The Artillery officers and men were very hard worked here, and it was obvious the very young soldiers of the Royal battery, which had lately arrived in the country, were unequal to the amount of physical labour entailed on working breaching guns under a burning sun. After twelve hours' duty behind the sand-bags, amidst the noise, smoke, and dust from the light sandstone worked up by the guns' recoil, one's back half broken by stooping to avoid getting one's head-dress ventilated by a bullet, or one's toes smashed by the guns, it was indeed an agreeable change to descend into camp, though one looked like a potter, and felt half baked. It was in this battery Lieutenant Moresby met his death by a round shot which struck his head.

The Portuguese cooks and their assistants had a particular objection to bring men's dinners here, and would, if shouted at, invariably throw down the cauldron of hot tea, or pile of dinners, and run. These cooks have had their natural history written by Dr. Buist. They are a regular institution in a regiment; very black, very greasy, one handkerchief around the head and another around the loins being all their clothing, always rejoice in the name of Jack, bear an amount of abuse and beating with the patience of a donkey, and get badly paid withal.

The breaching went on but slowly, for the round tower chosen was solid, and faced the rock, and its component stones were huge, and offered good resistance to the shot. Sometimes reports reached us of part of the garrison having left; at other times, that it had been reinforced. On the night of the 15th Lieutenant Dowker, with thirty sowars of the Hyderabad Contingent, brought in despatches from Sir Hugh Rose, who awaited our junction with him.

On the morning of the 16th the remainder of H. M.'s 86th Regiment marched into camp, with their band playing the British Grenadiers, and the same day the breach was reported practicable; but as we had been sold at Dhar, we expected a similar occurrence here. Two storming parties were told off: the Brigadier and Staff to accompany the one for the breach, composed of Royal Engineers, H. M.'s 86th, and 25th Regiment B. N. I.; and the other one, to be led by Captain Little, composed of H. M.'s 86th and men of his own gallant corps (the

25th). Assistant-Surgeon Sylvester was directed to accompany one storming party, and Assistant-Surgeon Cruickshank the other. Captain Little was directed to make a false attack, to draw away the concentrated resistance that might occur at the breach, but also, if practicable, to enter the fort. The spot chosen for this party was opposite the "Kattee Gattee," where the fort rock was not so steep but that it could be ascended, and where the wall was not very high. All attempts to prevent the garrison escaping, had they so willed it, would have been futile with our small Cavalry force, and in such a country; so that our Horse were left in charge of camp, which was struck.

Captain Keatinge, barefooted and noiseless, proceeded during the darkness to inspect the breach. Cautiously passing along the scarp of rock which connected our ridge of hills with the fort, he arrived within a few yards of the *débris* of the battered bastion; when an unexpected obstacle presented itself, in the shape of a deep trench cut in the rock, and extending completely across it, being some fourteen feet wide, and as many deep. But what signified this: the morrow was Saint Patrick's day, and the Royal County Downs were in the van.

On the 17th, at 3 A. M., we formed up in silence, ascended to the batteries, and just as grey dawn appeared one tremendous salvo from our guns, which hurled grape into the breach and shells and rockets into the fort, was the preconcerted signal for the stormers to rush on—and rush on they did, with a yell which of itself was terrible enough to affright anything in human form. Little, with his party, had succeeded in getting in simultaneously, or even before Keatinge and Gosset's party, at the breach. But our volley had roused the garrison, whose guns, being ready loaded and pointed, now gave us one equally astounding in return. Most of the round shot passed close over our heads with a frightful whirr-r-r. Scaling ladders were thrown across the cutting at the base of the breach, which in itself was as difficult to mount as could be well conceived ; but in went the gallant party, fighting hand to hand in the breach, and Keatinge fell severely wounded. Gosset was more fortunate : though shot twice through the helmet he escaped uninjured. Not so, many of the soldiery, who suffered severely, and ran on taking gun after gun—now shooting, now bayonetting the enemy, or dashing them over the height into the ravine below. One magazine blew up, and seven of the 86th were carried into the air : some were killed by the explosion, others horribly burnt. Their uniform, save the shoes, had been completely burnt away, and their bodies charred and blackened. The palace and buildings at the opposite end of the fort had still to be cleared, and by the time they were reached the great body of the enemy had escaped down through the town beneath, and were seen in full flight in the jungle beyond, for it was now bright daylight. Those that remained were shot or bayonetted. Major Orr, with a force of Cavalry, was stationed so as to intercept any fugitives that might escape in the direction the Brigadier considered the most likely to be taken by the garrison, and, as we subsequently learnt, accounted for many. In the night, Lieutenant Gowan, with a troop of Dragoons, went round to the opposite side of the fort, and at the signal for storming made a false attack by firing a number of rounds of blank ammunition ; but in other respects horsemen were useless at Chanderi. The fort was some four miles in circumference, and commanded a splendid view of the surrounding country. We captured a vast number of guns, and counted a hundred dead; and marched into camp through the deserted town, the bands playing, of course, St. Patrick's day.

The work of dismantling the fort was now commenced by Captain Fenwick and the Royal Engineers. Fortifications were thrown down, gates broken up, guns burst, but nothing valuable was found: the usual number of charpoys, water-vessels, heaps of grain and salt, with old, blood-stained clothes—this was all our prize, save the guns, which were of the rudest country manufacture: two brass ones were worth their metal. A garrison of Scindiah's men from Easaugurh was placed here to hold Chanderi, which they did until the enemy appeared there again some months after.

CHAPTER VI.

THE CENTRAL INDIA FIELD FORCE ARRIVES BEFORE JHANSI—INVESTMENT OF THE CITY—RIGHT AND LEFT ATTACKS—THE MAMELON—BATTLE OF THE BETWA—ASSAULT OF JHANSI—AFFAIR ON THE ROCK—JHANSI AFTER THE STORM—CAPTURE OF THE FORT—CLEARING THE GARDENS AND HOUSES—INTERIOR OF THE FORT—DISCOVERY OF THE REMAINS OF THE ENGLISH KILLED AT JHANSI.

ON the 19th, the 14th Dragoons left the 1st Brigade to join the 2nd, which had nearly reached Jhansi. The nearer that Force approached, the greater became the interest and excitement, for it was well known to all that the enemy was there in great force, and had made grand preparations for our reception. The country we marched through, in reaching the place, gave but little evidence of the change that had come over it since last traversed by Europeans. Excepting that few or no inhabitants were seen, the cultivation had been carried on as of old, and the fields were teeming with corn ripe for the sickle; but it seemed as though a plague had swept over the land, and carried off its occupants. The villages were deserted, and grass grew rank and untrampled in the streets; while the crane and long-legged wading birds, which love solitude, haunted the tanks and waters.

The aspect of Jhansi was imposing, standing as it did in bold relief on its hot and inhospitable-looking granite plain, from which sprang a few huge hills, and bald, woodless crags. (On one of these, situated 600 yards to the south-east of the fort, a vast number of the rebels were killed in attempting to escape after the city fell into our hands.) The city is situated amidst tanks and trees, has numbers of prominent buildings, and formed a great contrast to the barrenness round about it. It is entirely surrounded by a wall, which bore marks of recent repair, and measured about eleven miles in circumference: it was loopholed, and the bastions were mounted with guns. The fortress, huge and frowning, was situated on a rock overlooking the town, and was within the walls. Its deep, dark colour showed its antiquity, having been built by the Mahrattas a century ago. The remains of the European cantonment stood between us and the city, and verily it had been desolated. There were but the walls of houses, and most of these had been pulled down for the sake of the wood-work in them, and in the gardens vegetation had run wild. The sepoy huts had been destroyed by fire, and the rain had well nigh washed away all traces of the mud walls. The bells of arms and Star Fort, where Mr. Skene was said to have defended himself and wife, being of solid masonry, were left intact. The grave-yard, too, had been rifled of its tomb stones, its trees had been hewn down level with the ground, and the solemnity of the mounds under which lay some of England's dead had been disturbed.

The 2nd Brigade encamped in the plain some distance from Jhansi, but did not pitch tents. The enemy was visible in great numbers near the ruined bungalows intervening between us and the city. After the interchange of a few shots, and a sight of our Cavalry and Horse

Artillery, they retreated into the gardens near their defences, and the Major-General and Staff, with an escort, proceeded to reconnoitre their position, and, of course, attracted the fire of most of the enemy's batteries. They had placed guns on every bastion of the wall, and were said to have forty in position on the fort. One round tower, which mounted some very heavy pieces, had been recently rebuilt and washed white, so that it drew our artillery fire, and furnished so good a mark that it was ultimately knocked to pieces.

On the 23rd of March the place was thoroughly invested by our Cavalry. One large outpost, on the most distant side of the town, was under command of Major Gall, of the 14th K. L. D.; another, opposite the water palace, by Captain Thompson; Captain Forbes commanded one composed of the 3rd B. L. C.; and Captains Abbott, Murray, and Clerk, the posts of the Nizam's Cavalry. All egress or ingress to the besieged was at an end. There were prisoners taken at the pickets every night: one party from Calpee was captured bringing a convoy of rockets. The dauntless bravery of the Ranee was a great topic of conversation in camp. Far-seeing individuals thought they saw her under an awning on the large square tower of the fortress, where she was said to sit and watch the progress of the siege. Report told she was young and beautiful, and as yet unmarried. Field and opera glasses were constantly directed to the awning in question, over which hung sulkily a large red flag, destined shortly to give place to the one so dear to every Englishman.

The enemy, confining himself to his defences, and to some temples and trees near them, gave us an opportunity of approaching within gun-shot of the city, and to explore the houses and gardens, and speculate on the site of the brutal massacre which was rankling in our minds. One trace only at that time was seen—a woman's skeleton lay bleaching in the sun : the head was gone, and the remainder had been cleaned by beasts of prey. All trees and buildings likely to cover us, during our approach to the place, had been removed. But, our trenches once opened, batteries sprang into existence like mushrooms, in the night too, and each dawn added more voices to the unceasing chorus given out from the throats of our guns, howitzers, cohorns, and mortars. These were accumulated chiefly at two points of attack—one near the water palace, advantage being taken of some huge masses of loose rocks and remains of a fakeer's hut, and designated, by a finger post, "The Right attack;" the other was on a rock opposite their strongest outwork, though most vulnerable point, the Mamelon, and styled "The Left attack." Now the former place was not so decidedly uncomfortable—tents could be pitched there, and the fakeer's house in the mortar battery afforded shade and apparent, though not real, security from round shot; for on one occasion eight artillerymen were breakfasting there, when a cannon ball passed completely through the room, but injured no one.

On the night of the 29th we celebrated the anniversary of Mohumra with champagne, which re-called the memory of the days we spent on the bosom of the Euphrates in the most vivid and pleasing manner—in fact, we lived down here. It was always a busy spot, for there were gabions to be made, sand-bags to be filled, furnaces for heating shot requiring constant attention; and the relays of ammunition arriving, and reliefs of the infantry force, made this attack quite a preferable tour of duty. Advantage was taken of a height hard by, to erect a telegraph, which was worked by signal flags, and, in case of necessity, indicated to the flying outposts, " enemy escaping," " enemy advancing," and, like a weather vane, also the direction in which they might be coming or going, and was the signal for officers commanding outposts to " let slip the dogs of war." At night also, a shell was despatched into the city every few minutes, which occasionally fired their stacks of hay and forage, causing vast conflagrations, illuminating the city, and there were minor fires and flames resulting from the burning of the dead; and so the interest was kept up during the entire twenty-four hours.

No one considered the Left attack a desirable spot. Even George Robins would have been at a loss to point out a single advantage. Any one ran a considerable risk of being hit going in, and as great coming out, and almost as large a one when in the batteries. It was situated on a rising ground opposite their chief battery, the Mamelon, and very close to it there were no trees for shelter from the sun, and only large fragments of rock, well heated through, under which to take shelter from the enemy's fire

The men working the guns and mortars here were necessarily much exposed, and we lost a good many, chiefly gunners of the Hyderabad Contingent. Captain George Hare, commanding a regiment of infantry of that service, held this attack during the greater part of the siege. Any kind of ease, when not actually engaged, was totally out of the question. The rock was so hot no one could sit or lie on it without feeling scorched, and when standing upright the head of the individual was exposed to the enemy's fire. One of our elephants was hit, and many bullocks killed bringing in ammunition.

On the 24th of March the 1st Brigade joined us from Chanderi, and encamped about two miles from the other one, and a mile distant from the fort. General Whitlock, with the Saugor Field division, was daily expected to arrive and reinforce us, but never turned up.

After some days and nights of bombarding, the enemy's bastions began to look rugged, and their fire was less regular, and almost ceased through the night. Many of their most troublesome guns were silenced, particularly those on the new bastion of the fort; but they always managed to repair, though less completely every night, the damage we had done their chief outwork, the Mamelon, during the day, and seemed aware we should endeavour to make our entrance there. It was a very strong position, situated on a piece of elevated ground, with an abrupt slope towards us, and a gradual one inward towards the fort, and consisted of a half bastion, and was a continuation of the city ramparts, which were very high at this point, and crenellated, as at every other, for musketry. The muzzles of six guns peeped through the embrasures of the Mamelon: they were closed until the guns opened. Behind the pieces of Artillery was a *chevaux-de-frise*, and the embrasures were further strengthened by heavy piles and logs of wood. At the foot of the bastion in front, was a deep ditch of masonry, which we could not see until the position was assaulted. The distance between the enemy and ourselves here was very small. We could hear them talking, and see their uniform. They were regularly relieved night and morning, the exchange being made from a sallyport in the fortress near the Mamelon. At these times the 3rd Regiment of European Infantry, which occupied some fine temples near the spot where the Europeans were killed during the mutiny, harassed them with their Enfields pretty considerably. As the siege advanced, the investment was made more complete. The Cavalry pickets had guns and howitzers attached to them, and the one on the furthest side of the city had a body of hill-men or Gonds with it. They belonged to some Native State, and did good service, as well as the artillerymen who had been sent by the Begum of Bhopal. There were other motley troops, too, belonging to friendly Native States. All served to increase the singular mixture of soldiery before the besieged city, in which it was estimated forty lakhs of treasure awaited us. In the camp there was little excitement, being so far distant. On one occasion an attempt was made to move that of the second Brigade closer to the scene of action, but before the tents could be pitched round shot came rolling among them. The heat now began to increase considerably every day, and the hot winds, loaded with the red dust of the plains, set in.

On the night of the 30th a large force from both Brigades was suddenly ordered out, and led by the Major-General to the banks of the Betwa river, some six or seven miles from

Jhansi. An army of ten thousand men was reported to be arriving there. The second Brigade struck its camp, and remained on the alert throughout the night, to protect the standing camp of the first, now vacated.

On the morning of the 31st both camps were located together near the Telegraph hill. An hour afterwards, and the second Brigade moved towards the ruined jail, and the Madras and Bombay Sappers and Miners took up their quarters in a garden near the old sepoy lines. The force returned from the Betwa river, having met no enemy : and escalading was talked of and anxiously awaited.

The next evening, the two forces, including all but a handful of men to guard the camp, were ordered out, as we supposed, for another march to the river, but one under the Major-General bivouacked in rear of the second Brigade camp. The other, under Brigadier, now Sir C. Stuart, marched by a circuitous route towards the Betwa, and also bivouacked. During the night a horse or so of the Cavalry became loose, and charged through or near the sepoy element, on which, prone to excitement, a brisk discharge of their muskets ensued, which happily was attended with but few bad effects. One dragoon was wounded. Thus passed another sleepless night, hot and heavily.

Day had scarcely dawned when the videttes and pickets, which had been in our front during the night, began to fall back on us, and shortly afterwards, coming in grand array of battle over a rising knoll, was the army of the Peishwa, bent on raising the siege of Jhansi. Our General probably knew of their proximity, but we were not a little astonished. They brought up their long line of Artillery, supported by masses of Infantry and six or seven hundred Cavalry, and appeared to wish to turn our left. Having advanced within 600 yards of our line, they unlimbered and opened fire, which was very heavy. Sir Hugh Rose could not muster fifteen hundred men to oppose them, but all available troops were drawn up in line. In the centre of the first line were the heavy guns, supported by the 3rd Europeans, the 24th, and Hyderabad Infantry; on the right of the line a troop of 14th Dragoons, and one of Hyderabad Cavalry, with the Eagle troop H. A.; and on the left, Captain Lightfoot's field battery and two troops of H. M.'s 14th Dragoons. The troops which should have been our second and line of reserve, could they have been spared, consisted of Woolcombe's and Ommaney's battery, supported by H. M.'s 86th Regiment in the centre, and some Dragoons to their right, and on the left a troop of Hyderabad Cavalry and some Companies of the 25th Regiment. All left us about midnight, under the command of their Brigadier.

Our batteries now opened fire, and the Infantry on both sides blazed away furiously. The engagement became general, and was kept up with great spirit on both sides: the plains soon clouded with smoke; and the Artillery from both flanks of the line advanced, the Eagle troop to the right, so as to crush the enemy's gunners by an enfilading fire. In this movement one of the guns was knocked over and disabled, which gave the enemy great courage, and they manifested their delight by cheers; while their infantry fire began to tell on our close ranks around the heavy guns, and the men here were ordered to lie down The Horse Artillery gun having been disabled was more than could be borne, and Sir Hugh Rose directed Lieutenant Clarke, who commanded the Hyderabad Cavalry, to charge the enemy's battery, which was done, but ineffectually. Showers of grape, and volleys from the Velliattee matchlockmen, drove them back. Thrice the gallant Clarke charged, but with like effect. In fact, the enemy followed them up, and killed and wounded many men and horses, and wounded their leader severely. The battle was now brought to a speedy issue by the cavalry. The Major-General, at the head of Captain Need's troop of Dragoons, dashed into the enemy's left, while Prettyjohn and MacMahon led their troops into the enemy's right, and doubled them up. This was a magnificent sight, and in a moment the enemy's ranks were a mass of confusion : they were shaken and disorganised, and commenced a disastrous retreat. They were hurled back on the Betwa by the irresistible attack of the Dragoons. Occasionally the bravest amongst the rebels rallied, in a mass or *gole*, and fought hand to hand, as in the swamps about Dhar. The further they were pursued, the thinner and fewer they became, till at last little squares and groups and single fugitives dotted the plain. Six guns, with their ammunition waggons, were abandoned in their flight. Still our troops pressed onwards, unexpectedly coming on a second force, commanded by the Nana's agent, Tantia Topee, who ever preferred the rear. He now in turn opened his guns on our Cavalry, and threw both round shot and shell amongst us. Turnbull's and Lightfoot's batteries replied, and we saw this their second reserve force in full flight before us. Our cavalry and guns went after them at a killing pace, and caught them up at a small village near the river, which is broad, shallow, and stony here. Our guns again opened on them. They still had numbers of infantry with them : we had none, ours being unable to keep up : but we soon drove them across the river, in which they made great efforts to carry off their guns, ammunition, and elephants, but much of their ordnance fell into our hands here. The ardour of the Cavalry led them across the river into the burning jungle beyond, which was on fire from our shells. Captain Need, who was leading, dashed into the stream, and was quickly surrounded by the enemy. His horse, becoming frightened, would neither retreat nor go forward, and from this perilous position he was rescued by the gallantry of Captain Leith, of his Regiment, the 14th. The escape was miraculous, as nine sword-cuts were counted on the horse and trappings, yet not one touched Captain Need. For this act the Victoria Cross was awarded by Sir Hugh Rose, the only one given throughout the campaign; which fact, of course, induces the belief that very few men of valour could have existed in the Force. Still, daily acts of bravery were performed, which ordinary men appreciated.

But to accompany the very opportune movement of the 1st Brigade, which left us about midnight for another ford on the Betwa. It was led by Brigadier C. S. Stuart, and proceeded to Boregaum, and had just arrived when the battle in rear of the camp commenced, the heavy firing apprising them that the 2nd Brigade was engaged. Having reconnoitred the ford of Kolwar near, and finding no traçe of the enemy, the Brigadier retraced his steps to give assistance to Sir Hugh, if required, and in his return came on a number of the rebels flying for the ford. Lieutenant Giles, with thirty dragoons, cut them up. Many more would have been killed, but the rebel sepoys occupied some adjacent rocks and poured a brisk matchlock fire into the dragoons, killing one, and wounding five, as well as causing ten casualties among the horses. In advance of this place was the small village of Kooshabord, which three thousand of the enemy and six pieces of cannon had occupied, and these were opened on the line of Infantry as it advanced in skirmishing order. A few rounds of shell from Woolcombe's battery and the two guns R. A. caused them to commence a retreat; and the 86th and 26th Regiments, under Lieutenant-Colonels Robertson and Lowth, dashed forward and carried the place with the bayonet. During this attack, the Adjutant, Cochrane, of the 86th Regiment had his own and two troop horses belonging to wounded men in the 14th Dragoons shot under him. The enemy now began to retire, fighting, and though Lieutenant Giles exhibited the most dauntless gallantry, with the thirty men, now reduced by six, and ten horses—and seconded, as he was, too, by some Hyderabad Horse—he could do literally nothing against the dense masses of matchlockmen save cut up outsiders. The ground, too, was impracticable for Artillery, and our tired-out Infantry could not long keep up with the fugitives, and the pursuit was at length abandoned.

This was one of the numerous instances during the campaign where a thousand light and well-equipped horse, with their hearts in the work, would have been quite invaluable to Sir Hugh Rose, and would have inflicted a most decisive blow on the flying hordes. As it stood, it was supposed that two hundred and fifty had fallen, and many more were severely wounded. The six guns, two elephants, some camels, ammunition, and treasure, were captured, making a total of eighteen guns and two standards left in our hands by Tantia Topee ; besides which, fifteen hundred dead were scattered on the plains of the Betwa in this the first and greatest battle which occurred throughout his sanguinary and ill-starred career. The tired troops retraced their steps, having beaten 10,000 men without a single man being withdrawn from the batteries, or from the Cavalry outposts and flying camps surrounding the town.

Why the garrison did not make a sortie, and destroy our batteries, while the Peishwa's army was attempting their rescue from without, it is impossible to imagine. Their overpowering numbers must have been successful, however well our Infantry and Gunners might have stood to their guns. They may have been deterred by a false attack made by Major Gall and Captain Field, R. A., on a distant part of the city wall.

On the 2nd of April the Force had a day of comparative rest, and the enemy's park of Artillery was drawn up before the tents of the Major-General—twenty pieces of ordnance in all, with tumbrils and ammunition waggons. It was a goodly sight.

Early on the following morning every one was silently roused, and fell in to assault the city. It was kept a secret until after midnight, from most of the Force. The stormers consisted of H. M.'s 86th Regiment, 21st Co. R. Engineers, Bombay and Madras Sappers, 3rd European Regiment, and 25th Native Infantry. These were divided into three parties: the County Downs and 25th were to assemble in the left attack, and go in at the breach, while the 3rd Europeans and remaining troops were to rush on from the right attack in two parties. The order was short, detailing the order of troops and their leaders, who were to start at a signal of three guns fired in succession by Captain Ommaney, and plant their scaling ladders against the ramparts at places indicated ; and as the Major-General had no knowledge of the interior of the city, the troops were told it was desirable to make for the Ranee's palace. All being ready, the signal was waited for in breathless anxiety. We fancied there was some little delay in it, for it began to get light. The columns had some way to go from the right attack, and the enemy must have been aware of their approach, for they had manned the ramparts, and opened a murderous fire, but nothing could excel the ardour of the stormers, cheering as they rushed forward across a field and then down a road ; but here the Sappers began to fall thick and fast, while the roaring of the enemy's fort guns now became something terrific, and for a moment, to gain breath, the party take advantage of the shelter of some ruins. Another dash, and the walls are reached, and up go the ladders amid a hail of bullets, rockets, huge stones, and every possible description of missile. Up go three ladders, with "Hurrah !" Lieutenants Dick, Meiklejohn, and Fox, are on the rampart, but, alas! the crush of men to follow breaks the ladders, and these three gallant fellows fall—the two former killed, and

Fox severely wounded, and dying. All were thrown into confusion, being now at the mercy of the garrison, when a Lieutenant of Engineers calls for the powder bag, carries it by the help of a few Sappers, and under a hail of bullets fixes it to a postern gate, fires it, and out flies the door in fragments. A rush is made into the cloud of smoke to get through the entrance, but even that fails—it is filled by huge blocks of stone and masonry. Nothing remains now but to bring away the dead and wounded. All helped in the sad task, and the dispirited columns moved back to the rifle pits.

The stormers from the left were more fortunate. They flew over the few yards between them and the breach, and then found a large trench of masonry at its foot. To jump into this, and plant the ladders, was but the work of a moment, and up they went, young Dartnell first gaining the breach, when the men from their impetuosity broke the ladder, and for a moment left him alone, to be hacked at by the demons within. He was very badly wounded, and only saved his life by protecting his head from their sabre cuts with his arm, which suffered frightfully. These stormers were eminently successful. They gained the Mamelon, slaying all they found there, and ran down the incline to the street leading to the palace, which street ran close under the fort walls. The matchlock and musketry fire on the men at this point was perfectly hellish! The bullets fell so thickly in the dusty road, that they resembled the effect of hailstones falling in water when striking it, and the men fell thick and fast here. One point of the street ran quite close to the gateway of the fort, and was not passed without severe loss. Here it was that most of our men fell, while being led by Captain Darby, of the County Downs, who was also severely wounded. It was at this spot, too, Dr. Stack of that Regiment was killed, and two other medical officers wounded. These devoted fellows had actually to halt here to drag the wounded under the shelter of an adjacent wall. Shouts of triumph rang through the city, the enemy all made a rush for the fortress, and left the walls free for the stormers, who came in and joined in the street fighting. There was the Major-General and staff, utterly heedless of danger, leading the men on to the palace. Some Horse Artillery guns were brought in, and poor Major Turnbull was mortally wounded. The palace was found full of sowars, who fought until they met their death. The Grenadier Company of the 3rd European Regiment, and some of H. M.'s 86th soldiers, broke down a wall, and endeavoured to attack them in flank; but this mode failed, and they charged straight at them, bayonetted them, and took their ready-saddled horses, and some English colours, one of which was immediately hoisted on the palace by Captain Darby, under a heavy fire from the Fort, the guns of which were now turned on the city. The Ranee had fled to the Fort, apparently but shortly before, probably as soon as the noise of the assault alarmed her. An unfortunate explosion of gunpowder, similar to that of Chanderi, took place, and again some five or six of the 86th were horribly burnt. The street fighting, or rather house fighting, went on until nearly nightfall. About 3 P. M. four hundred of the enemy sallied out, and were apparently going for Tehree, when part of the force left in the camp of the 1st Brigade, consisting of Woolcombe's battery, some companies of the 24th N. I. and Hyderabad Contingent Infantry, with a handful of dragoons, went out to attack them. The rebels then took shelter on an isolated rock with paths or shelves on it, and were surrounded and shelled. Many preferred lying down on their powder-flasks, and blowing themselves up. Finally the Infantry went up and cleared it, killing the four hundred, who fought to the last. We lost one officer, Lieutenant Parke, of the 24th N. I., and had one wounded. Ten or twelve men also were killed and wounded at the attack. Altogether, it was one of the most successful in the campaign. Our number of killed and wounded at the battle of the Betwa and subsequent assault was about two hundred and eighty.

There was one individual whose attention to the wounded and dying must have attracted every one's notice. He was always present by night or by day, regardless of danger: he seemed animated but by one desire, which was to do good and afford consolation to the dying, whether Catholic or Protestant. This was the Rev. Mr. Strickland. He, too, will reap his reward.

So soon as the fighting had ceased, officers and men began to look about them with that spirit of curiosity which pervades one when visiting the shops in Wardour Street, Leicester Square: they dived into every house and searched its dark corners, they pulled down walls, or parts of walls, which looked of recent build, all in this self-same spirit of curiosity—not to *loot*, of course, because that was forbidden under the strictest punishment. One class of articles, however, seemed to me to be looked on as fair loot by even the most scrupulous—these were the gods found in the temples. They were collected in great numbers, and were strangely sought after by every officer and soldier. There were Gunputties and Vishnoos innumerable, and of every metal. Some were really pretty ornaments, silver, with gold bangles on their grotesque limbs, and small enough to be worn on the watch chain; others were of brass and stone, of rare workmanship: and so general had the rebellion been in this city, that even the fakeers and Gossains had left their holy places, and armed against us. These researches, as is generally the case, were prosecuted under some disagreeables: the stench from the dead was horrible, while the gases liberated during putrefaction had given an elephant's bulk to the horses, and had magnified the men into giants' proportions. Numbers of the enemy were still hiding; hoping to find an opportunity to escape. The chief interest centred in and about the fortress, and palace of the Ranee. This latter building was of a square shape, enclosing a large court-yard. It faced a narrow street, and its outer walls were covered by native paintings, illustrating state processions, war, marriages, and the chase, in all which huge elephants, prancing horses, and people with big eyes and sharp noses, figured extensively. Inside the building were pet animals of all kinds, indigenous and brought from afar—white elephants, spotted deers, antelopes, gazelles, dogs, monkeys, pigeons, parrots, and cockatoos. Everything was in the greatest confusion and disorder, and the yard strewn with clothes, firearms, horse and elephant gear, cooking utensils, grass, grain, and the litter of horses. The staircase leading to the upper stories scarce admitted a man of portly figure, and was so low that one crouched to ascend. The first story, when gained, had a very handsome appearance—in fact, was somewhat gorgeous. The chief apartments ran the whole length of the palace front, the suite consisting of a large durbar room, two sleeping apartments, an inner *sans-souci*-looking sort of chamber, the ceiling of which was of plate-glass mirrors, the walls were of carving and gilded panels, and also ornamented by mirrors and paintings; the floor was spread with one vast cushion of wool or cotton, covered with crimson velvet, so that one's feet sank in its embraces as if in snow. Here one pictured the Ranee taking her mid-day ease, or listening to her favorite minstrel and the twang-twang of his guitar. The large room was also beautiful—painted, glazed, and ornamented, carpeted by rugs of Persian manufacture, lit by four large windows, reaching from the ceiling to the ground, and at night by large chandeliers of purple glass. It was furnished with chairs and ottomans, tables and couches, with pictures and ornaments in abundance, many of costly metal. The sleeping rooms were fitted up by one no novice in luxuries, and ornamented like the preceding ones, the colours of scarlet and gold prevailing. The bedsteads were of pure silver, and the furniture and coverlets of scarlet satin, silk, and gold: women's dresses, and some very full skirts with gilt trimmings, doubtless belonging to nautch girls, were lying about. Everything betokened the hasty, and probably unexpected, flight of the Ranee. It looked somewhat strange to see groups of sunburnt men, in red coats, with powder-besmeared faces, prowling about, their bayonets yet wet with blood. Along the passages and verandahs of the palace were thousands of brass and copper vessels, some of such huge proportions that it suggested to one the idea that they must have been making elephant curries, or accustomed to feeding on a Brobdignagian scale. These alone were very valuable, and must have been an enormous item in the prize account. Then there were some horribly dark-looking rooms, bringing the Italian dungeons forcibly to mind : these appeared to be a sort of store-rooms for an indescribable variety of articles. "Rubbish shot here" should have been written over the entrances. In the smaller upper rooms the valuables were found, consisting of shawls, scarfs, turbans, gold ornaments, jewels, and silver vessels, together with bags of rupees and gold mohurs. But the oot was not all found in one place, or at one time. Other chests of treasure were constantly being discovered by the help of the divining rods of the Prize Agents. Some English plate was recovered, which had belonged to some of the victims of the massacre. Guards were placed over all the treasure, some of the staff took up their abode in the palace, and the town was held by Infantry and guns.

The enemy had retired into the fortress, on which their flag was still hanging. They kept up a desultory fire from their guns, and shot at all they saw from the loopholes. It was thought they would hold out in the fort some time, and it became rather a knotty question how they were to be got out : the place was wondrously strong. Breaching, sapping, and such like processes were discussed, but as the Engineers had no plan of the building, any process would have been doubtful. On the night of the assault none of the enemy escaped, but on the night following, they sallied out of the fort, the Ranee and attendants accompanying them. They must have divided into small parties outside the city before they reached our line of videttes, and so have stolen through them. The parties opposite Major, now Colonel, Gall's pickets were thrice driven back, and there was considerable firing at that part of the city out-skirt. The great body appears to have gone through the line without much annoyance. In strategy of this kind the cowardly Asiatic excels. Great numbers must have been driven back, and their escape altogether prevented, for on the following day they were found in small bodies occupying the houses and temples situated in gardens on the environs of the city, and some very severe fighting ensued, causing us great loss.

The escape of the enemy was only known at daybreak. A picket of the 86th Regiment, being near the gateway of the fort, saw it was open, and as the men were not fired on, they cautiously approached, and finally, with some officers, entered, and found it evacuated to a man. The red flag now gave place to the Union Jack. The Major-General, with Horse Artillery and Cavalry, gave instant pursuit, but the Ranee had too great an advantage in the start, and with her retainers got clear away, and we heard little more of her until our arrival before Calpee. Lieutonant Dowker, however, was near them at one time, and disturbed the Ranee at her morning meal. Had he not been wounded, he would probably have overtaken her. While the pursuit was going on, the Infantry and Artillery were busily engaged in clearing the houses of bodies of the enemy, who had now become desperate. Shells were dropped from the roofs into rooms below ere they would come out ; and most of the buildings being crenellated, were capable of a good defence. It was in this work Captain Sinclair, of the Hyderabad Contingent, was killed, and Lieutenants Simpson, Lewis, and Fowler, most seriously wounded ; besides many men killed and wounded. Some of the more desperate took to the open, and tried to escape, but the Cavalry did their work nobly, and on one side of the city, at and near the outposts, were piles of dead.

> "The rice fields, where the tufted stalks grow green round tepid pools,
> "Were trodden red by flying crowds of unbelieving fools.
> "The bright canals that girt the town as with a silver net,
> "Were scarlet with the slain Moors' blood—the melons purple wet."

It took several days to clear the place completely. During the whole siege the greatest forbearance was shown to all who would peacefully surrender, and yet the estimated number of killed was four thousand: in fact, there was an amount of forbearance and Christian kindness displayed by the Europeans to unfortunate women and children, and to aged men, that reflected more credit on their already lustrous arms, and would not have been exhibited by any other European nation under the circumstances which caused the appearance of a British Force before the walls of Jhansi. It is no fiction when it is said the soldier shared his meals with some of the people found destitute in the city; and many of the women, I believe, joined the English camp.

If the fortress from the outside looked strong, the inside appeared much stronger, to the most inexperienced eye. The strength of the entrance was visible—steep, and winding through gate after gate, each division of the passage enfiladed by the one above, the walls thickly loopholed for matchlockmen and armed with jinjal and wall pieces, beside traversing guns. One dismounted gun of enormous dimensions lay in the gateway: it looked like one of the large pipes of the Vehar Water Works, and would have burst with a smaller charge. On gaining the interior the cause of their speedy evacuation became obvious—there was *no water*. The large tank which lay beneath the curtain it was said would have been breached had the enemy remained, was dry. A great part of the interior of the fort was occupied by the citadel, and this was surmounted by a high flag-staff tower, with terraced roof, the view from which was most perfect and extensive. The enemy must have been able to count every tent, and with a telescope (many were found in the fort) descry all our movements and the exact site of our pickets: the excitement which must have prevailed here when Tantia's army came to their rescue it would be impossible to imagine, and their proportionate chagrin as they saw it fly in disorder before our Dragoons. The havoc of our shot and shell was terrific, and great execution must have been done by these missiles. It was said 400 per diem met their death by them. They had torn through roofs, and rent the floors, and penetrated into almost every nook of the place. It was here the great bulk of the property taken from the European residents of Jhansi was found: it was all huddled together in motley mass, with grain, and salt, and sugar.

There were books by the cartload, and their former owners' names in them, writing desks, ladies' work boxes, stationery, apparel of Europeans of both sexes, and the toys of innocent children who had shared the common fate, boxes of medicines, guitars, telescopes, surgeons' instruments, macassar oil, looking glasses—in fact, the list was endless. There was a large number of the huge brass and copper cauldrons also, and I don't know how many pieces of ordnance, or how much ammunition. But the citadel had none of the splendour of the palace. It seemed to have been given up to the rebel soldiery.

Near the fortress were the remains of the vast ricks of grass which the enemy had stored for his Cavalry. Our shells had reduced them to a stratum of ashes. There were hundreds of cartloads of fuel also, and of this much remained. In the arsenal were piles of shot in abundunce, and the skeletons of some English carriages, the wood and leather work burnt : and as some of the houses were still smouldering, it made men wary in approaching places where shot was stacked, powder being, in our minds, associated with them. The city was placed under military rule, the Cavalry outposts still remained surrounding it, and Major Robertson was made commandant, and the civilians took up their abode in the water palace of the Ranee.

On the 12th of April the head quarters of H. M.'s 14th Dragoons, and of the 86th Regt., joined the Force, and the outposts of Cavalry came in ; and it began to be rumoured we were to march on Calpee. The Kotah mutineers, who had eluded General Roberts, marched on Sipree, in our rear, with a large amount of treasure. At this time the grave was discovered where the remains of the English residents who were killed had been buried. It was outside the city wall, near the Mamelon battery. Advantage seems to have been taken of some stone pits which existed there, and they were apparently all buried together. It was the Major-General's wish to re-inter them, but this the Engineers found impracticable. The pits were opened, and the sight was well calculated to inspire the soldiery with a desire for rude bloodshed.

Unripened by intellectual art, many an one stole away a fragment of the garment which encircled the hallowed remains of those who lay there ; and one tender subaltern, who was much affected until evening, caused us some merriment by giving rise to what newspapers would style "a moving incident." He was observed to be unusually quiet at mess, and to have something concealed in the breast of his stable-jacket. After much pressing, he was induced to produce the object he appeared to cherish so dearly. It proved to be a bone, which he had taken from the grave, and promised in his heart to carry to England, and let it rest in its native soil. Alas ! that so fine a sentiment and commendable intention should resolve itself into a joke ! but the Assistant-Surgeon of the Regiment, horribly material in his ideas, pronounced the relic to be the shank-bone of a leg of mutton !

Before we left Jhansi a barrier of stones was placed to mark the sacred spot, and the Rev. Mr. Schwabe and the Rev. Mr. Strickland performed the burial rites over the sleepers, a large portion of the Force, and its Staff, attending; and it now remains to mark the spot by some lasting memorial. Our wounded were placed in the citadel and palace, under the care of Dr. Ritchie, Field Surgeon.

CHAPTER VII.

THE FIELD FORCE MARCHES TO BEDORA—MAJOR GALL'S VICTORY AT LOHAREA—THE BRIGADES MARCH ON CALPEE—THE HEAT—ACTION OF KOONCH—COUP DE SOLIEL—SIMOON—SCARCITY OF WATER—OUR LINE OF MARCH.

ON the 18th, in consequence of intelligence received from Colonel Wetherall, who was on his road to join the Major-General's Staff, a Field Force marched at midnight to attack a fort some thirty miles distant, which was occupied by some of the Chanderi rebels. It consisted of half the Bombay 4—2 Battery, 50 Sowars H. C., a wing 3rd Bombay Cavalry, and 25th N. I., together with a large howitzer manned by Royal gunners. The whole was commanded by Colonel Louthe, of H. M.'s 86th Regiment. This force halted on reaching the village of Bedora, having met Col. Wetherall and his escort. They had passed the fort we were sent out to attack, and found it evacuated.

On the 19th the wing of the 3rd Bombay Cavalry left us, and marched towards Goonah to form a junction with the 71st Highlanders who were coming up the road to join the Force. While this Field Force was sent in this direction, Major Orr was sent to clear the road from Jhansi to Chickaree, and from thence northward to Goorserai, proceeding to Kotra. In this service, one Fert, near the river Betwa, with a garrison of forty men, and three pieces of cannon, surrendered to him. A third Field Force, under Major Gall, consisting of a squadron of H. M.'s 14th Light Dragoons, Lightfoot's Battery, some companies of the 3rd European Regiment, and of the 25th, together with a few Hyderabad sowars was dispatched on the Calpee road; and while encamped at the village of Loharea, nine miles N. W. of Poonch, the villagers betrayed one of the sowar outpost to some of the rebel Cavalry, who surrounded them, and the Nizam's Troopers had to cut their way out. Major Gall, therefore, surrounded Loharea by day-break on the 5th of May, and sent to the chief of the garrison to desire him to surrender—a chieftain by name Monohur Singh. His retinue came out, but the garrison, numbering one hundred and fifty men, preferred fighting, and took possession of a small fort built of bricks and dried mud. Major Gall now placed a couple of guns and two howitzers in position, outside a ditch and second line of works which surrounded the fort. Lieutenant Armstrong, with two companies of his corps, the 3rd Europeans, took advantage of a sort of guard-house near the ditch, and from thence advanced to the gateway of the fort, and without difficulty forced open two doors guarding the entrance; but the enemy were behind the third, and stopped all further progress until Lieutenant Bonus, of the Engineers, repaired to the village, and found an old pair of bellows, which he charged with sixty pounds of gunpowder and hung on the door, and fired it. This opened the way for the stormers, and in they went, the 3rd Europeans led by Donne and Newport, and the 25th men by Rose, while Fenwick made a false attack on the south side. It was a bloody hand-to-hand fight. Fifty-seven mutineers were killed in the gateway, and thirty-three in the interior, making a total of ninety. One hundred and fifty small arms were taken, and one brass gun, together with drums, bugles, and plates bearing the number of the 12th Bengal Infantry. It was a most successful affair, attended with the small loss of one killed and twelve wounded: of these two were officers, Lieutenants Donne and Newport of the 3rd Europeans.

On the 24th, Colonel Lowth's Field Force returned to Jhansi, the Brigades were under orders to march, sales were held every morning, and Serjeant-Major Hunt sold much of the captured jewellery and gold, besides shawls, scarfs, and turbans, by public auction, under the superintendence of Lieutenant Strutt, one of the prize-agents. The spirited bidding was wonderful, and real cashmere shawls (made in England) sold at great prices!

On the following day, at midnight, the 1st Brigade and Staff of the Force left for Calpee, and on the 2nd of May the 2nd Brigade followed, leaving Colonel Liddle of the 3rd Europeans with the Head Quarter Wing of his corps to command at Jhansi: he had besides a few Cavalry and Artillery, and a strong body of convalescent wounded men and officers. After leaving

Jhansi the heat became fearful: the hot wind blew day and night, and, as our thirst increased, the stock of beer and drinking luxuries became rapidly lessened, and there were few officers who had anything besides water or Commissariat arrack to drink. Metal articles, even in a double-roofed tent, became so hot, that it was with difficulty the hand could be kept in contact with them. I had heard of mutton chops being cooked in that way, and imagined I should soon be able to perform the operation. The country we marched through was flat, and without vegetation. A few miserable trees of camel-thorn and prickly pear existed near the villages. The dust was several inches thick on the roads, and, being so disturbed by the advance of the column, rose in such blinding clouds during the still night, that a regular coat formed over men and horses, and at day-break the former looked like so many pantaloons with painted faces and powdered hair: it produced a feeling of suffocation and thirst, which, combined with drowsiness, induced by the very slow pace of a large column, rendered marching by far the most disagreeable part of the campaign. Including halts, the pace could not have averaged two miles an hour. The heat during the day obliged us to march every night, and almost the whole night through, leaving but one or two hours for sleep, which was perfectly out of the question in the day, the attempt produced such a feeling of fullness in the head, making one fearful of apoplexy: many of the soldiers who slept during the time the sun shone never woke again, and were found dead. The further the column marched the scarcer became the water: it was now only found in small round wells of very great depth, and at the halt near a well, the noise and demand for water was distressing. The Bheestee's bullock became as great an object of veneration to a soldier as it would have been to a Brahmin. The water one drank was lukewarm, and often had a brackish flavour. The duty of rear guard officer became the bugbear of the subalterns of the Force: there was an interminable amount of baggage, each officer having ten times more than necessary, even on a liberal allowance, and a hundred times more than Sir Charles Napier's code allowed. The rear guard could never leave until all was gone from the encamping ground, and this took some hours to clear, so that they always had a few hours in the sun in addition to a disturbed night.

On the 3rd of May the Head Quarter Wing of the 71st Highland Light Infantry joined us, with their Band and Bagpipes, and the sound of these at starting, and on gaining our encamping ground, was the only cheering thing which happened during the 24 hours. Their dress and equipment was almost perfect—a loose holland blouse and overalls of Kakee dye, and a light shako-shaped hat, with cover and curtain of the same colour. The 3rd B. Europeans were dressed much in the same way, but were a forage cap, and pugry, which afforded little protection, and hung dabby and flabby down the neck.

On the 5th of May, the two Brigades joined at the village of Pucha; and on the night of the 6th the assembly was sounded at 9 P. M., and the Force marched at 10. We heard there was a large body of the enemy sixteen miles ahead of us, at a town called Koonch, in the district of Jaloun, and situated on the road from Calpee to Gwalior, distant 42 miles south-west of the former city. On the arrival of the 2nd Brigade, at day-break, the town, being yet about a mile distant, appeared of good size, and entirely surrounded by trees. An old fort looking out of the midst of them could be distinguished, mounting the red flag ; so that it was evident the enemy was there. In fact, Major Gall discovered by reconnaisance that the greater part of the Calpee Sepoys, the Kotah Cavalry, the Bundeelahs of the Ranee of Jhansi, and other disaffected landholders, were in the city, and commanded by Tantia Topee and the Ranee in person. The 2nd Brigade, with the Major-General, was on our left, but on the opposite side of the town, and Major Orr's Nizam's Force was on our right. The heat at this early hour was intense, and the mirage most remarkable. The whole of the surrounding country was dried up and covered with light brown soil, and perfectly flat, yet it appeared one beautiful lake of water, and the few trees assumed the appearance of gigantic height ; and when Major Orr's Force approached, so distorted was it, that we could not tell whether it was friend or foe. The horses appeared twenty feet high, and riders in proportion, and the heated air currents, ascending, made them tremulous and crooked, and we formed up for action until we discovered who they were. The men had their grog served out to them, and were allowed time to get their morning meal.

As we approached, the day's proceedings commenced by a heavy cannonade, which the 1st Brigade, under the Major-General, had opened on the rebel Cavalry, which could be seen at the outskirts of the trees surrounding Koonch. Along the entire length of the city, on the side facing us, were gardens enclosed by high mud walls, and behind these were dense masses of Infantry, and guns placed at intervals. These defences were battered by the heavy guns, which caused the enemy to reply to our fire. We were then at too great a distance to be harmed by them. The 2nd Brigade formed up in line opposite a small, village, and, with the exception of one advance in skirmishing order made by the 71st Highlanders, did little but remain grilling under the enemy's fire throughout the greater part of the day. It was wretched to see how these men felt the heat, even though many of them had gone through the Crimean campaign. Seven died on the field, and many were struck down, and with difficulty recovered. This had a depressing effect on the others, who seemed to be in momentary dread of sharing the same fate; whilst the 3rd Bombay European Regiment, on their right, in line, seemed more annoyed by their useless Enfield rifles than by the sun. No amount of force exerted by the men would drive the bullets down to the breech of their weapons. Lieuteuant-Colonel Gall now rode across our front with a few dragoons, and entered the gardens, where he saw vast bodies of their infantry and cavalry. This officer seemed to enjoy a *carte blanche* from the enemy to go as near them as he chose without being fired on, and, if under fire, never to be injured. It was a most extraordinary fact, that though exposing himself to fire more than any officer in the force, he served through the entire campaign without a scratch, until he became thoroughly worn out at Gwalior, by unceasing exertions and exposure to the sun. The further inactivity of the 2nd Brigade was varied by seeing a most dashing movement made on our left front by Major Orr and the Contingent force. This officer had already fought his way from his encampment at Aite to the village of Omree, and drove back a large Cavalry and Artillery force that had gone out to oppose his advance. Arrived at Omree, he sent his infantry to storm the wall and gardens in his front, which they did, and drove them out on our right, when Lieutenant Dowker charged them. It was with considerable chagrin the men and officers of the 2nd Brigade, who were impatient to take their share in the fight, witnessed the Contingent Infantry again driven out of the gardens by overpowering numbers, without being permitted to go to their assistance. The enemy grew bold from this temporary advantage they had gained, and opened a heavy fire on the Nizam's guns, pitching their shrapnell into the very midst of them.

Presently we saw red-coats in the old fort, and thought them enemies until the red flag gave place to the Union Jack. Sir Hugh had gone in with the County Downs and 25th, in skirmishing order, supported by the Horse Artillery, field batteries, and Dragoons on the flank. Lieutenant Colonel Lowth commanded the line of reserve, consisting of Dragoons, Woolcombe's battery, and half the 86th Regiment. It was but the work of ten minutes, and Major Steuart had planted the 86th colours on the fort. As soon as this appeared, the Cavalry, Horse

Artillery, and field battery—which became horse artillery for the occasion, and went nearly as fast—dashed away from the infantry and heavy guns of the 2nd Brigade, in a few moments unlimbered, and blazed into the masses of rebel infantry, now swarming out of the town and gardens into the open plain. This was, with the exception of the battle of the Betwa, the only time I ever saw the rebels entirely at our disposal in the open plain, and I began to fancy we should now exterminate them; but I had not taken the exhausted state of our men and animals into account. Pitman, with the Bombay field battery, and Crowe, with the horse artillery, were up with the rebels in a few minutes, and poured volleys of grape into the retiring masses. Contrary to my expectation, however, the enemy did not retire in any confusion, but fought most gallantly, throwing out masses or clusters of sixty or a hundred men to cover their retreat. So eager were the artillerymen, and so rapidly did they load and fire, that it was difficult to make them cease, that the cavalry might charge—in fact, they might have fired longer with advantage. The enemy's column was scarcely sufficiently broken for cavalry to cut them up. Captain MacMahon and Captain Blythe, each leading their troops of the 14th Dragoons, charged magnificently, but about four hundred yards of heavy ploughed land intervened between the troop led by the former officer and the enemy's covering party. This somewhat checked the pace of the troop, and at the same moment the rebel band delivered a volley into the front rank: four men were killed outright and many horses, several others were wounded, and altogether a great number of saddles were emptied. Each of the rebels was provided with a Government musket, belt, and cartouch box, in capital order, and well provided with cartridges. After firing, down went the musket and out came the sharp-cutting native sword: they evidently could not use the bayonet. They cut and slashed our horses and men so long as one of their band remained alive. I counted thirty-six regular sepoys lying dead at that spot. To show the force with which they cut with their native swords, it is only necessary to instance Line Sergeant Wilson, who had his bridle arm completely severed above the elbow, and on another occasion the thigh of a Gond was cut through at one blow. On the other hand, I have seen the blunt sword of a dragoon bound off the skull instead of cleaving it ; while on the same day a native cut off part of a dragoon's foot, shoe, sole, and all ! I have seen a dragoon cut a man across the face with sufficient force to slice the top of his head off, yet he scarcely cut through the cheek bones. But in spite of all this inferiority of arms, exhausted and almost dying as half the force was, we drove them before us in indecent haste on the Ooraii road, killed five hundred, and took nine guns and a quantity of ammunition. Captain Abbott led his men on with his usual praiseworthy valour, and showed that in a pursuit no weapon equals the spear.

In this action, nothing could have been more praiseworthy than the valour displayed by the sepoys of the late Bengal Army, and nothing more disgraceful than the behaviour of the Cavalry, who, in every fight I saw, distinguished themselves signally by cowardice. Tantia Topee's "order-book" was found subsequently at Calpee, and, singularly enough, the last order in it expressed his thanks to the spirit of bravery which animated his men at Koonch, and that if they would only fight so a few times more, the infidel English would be exterminated. There were other matters of interest in it. One man, for crime, had been condemned to death by sentence of a court martial, but the sentence was remitted to a year's imprisonment, and signed "Nana Sahib," &c., and another. His offence was, that, on being ordered on a march to Banda to escort treasure, he ventured to offer the very sensible suggestion, that there was none to be had if he went there. On the field, during the pursuit, the body of a beautiful woman lay: she had died recently, and probably from exhaustion and thirst. She attracted much attention, and it was rumoured to be the Ranee, but the Ranee was not half so handsome. The 1st Brigade, Cavalry and Horse Artillery, had to gallop through the town ere they came up with the enemy, and joined somewhat later in the pursuit. Those that were able followed up the rebel army to a village about seven miles distant, when the horses could go no further. It was reported that ten horses had died of thirst and exhaustion in one battery alone. The scorching wind blew with the force of an English March wind the entire day. The long train of sick in ambulances and dhoolies were of course unavoidably exposed : no tents could be pitched, but they congregated round wells, and were tolerably well off for water. Sir Hugh Rose suffered much from the sun, and was obliged to dismount for a time and seek shade, when he was attended by Dr. Vaughan, and subsequently resumed his duties.

The day's fighting and pursuit were only just ended when night came on ; and it was so dark that many of us could not find the lines marked out by the Quarter Masters, nor could we find water, so that we remained holding our horses until day broke, suffering from parching thirst. The hot wind did not abate the whole night, and our horses had not had a mouthful the day previous, so that daylight was doubly welcome, when we encamped, and both Brigades took a day of rest, which was much needed.

At two A. M. of the 9th, the Major-General moved off with the 1st Brigade to follow up his success, and inflict another blow on the enemy if possible ere he reached Calpee ; but his column was obliged to halt at Hurdowi, one march distant. The fort at this place was previously occupied, but evacuated by the enemy when Sir Hugh advanced, and the chief, an important character, surrendered. It was most extraordinary to observe how climacteric influences worked against our speedy progress towards the holy Jumna. The 2nd Brigade had been directed to follow the other on the following day, but about 4 P. M. the sky, usually so bright, became thick and mud-coloured, as though the air was filled by immense clouds of insects, and the heat was suffocating. This appearance rapidly increased for an hour, when it blew a regular hurricane. The wind was charged with sand, which being driven with such velocity well nigh blinded us: even the horses crouched under it, and became quite frightened. The wind roared as it does at sea, and in a few moments there was scarce a tent left of the vast town of canvas, which had stood on the plain but a moment before. Many of the tents were rent in pieces, and the consternation was great: one scarce knew what was the next freak nature would play us. This state of things lasted for fifteen minutes, during which time breathing became difficult. After the wind had subsided a little in violence much rain accompanied it (each drop was nectar to the thirsting souls on whom it fell), and the temperature cooled down suddenly, and remained so until night, proving greatly refreshing to those who were suffering from the exposure during the action.

Unfortunately, even this small fall of rain had made the tents so heavy that our march onward was postponed until the following day, the 10th, when we advanced to the village of Ooraii. Here we found a tank of muddy water, but that was a luxury. Ooraii appeared to be a larger village than we usually saw in these parts. Previous to the mutiny, two companies of Bengal Infantry were stationed here, and three European bungalows were now in ruins. Just as we were about to encamp, a sowar brought a dispatch from Sir Hugh Rose, directing the Brigade to march on Banda, which was on the direct road to Calpee. The Major-General marched to Succalee, in order to turn the defences which the enemy had placed on the high road, and to join Colonel Maxwell, who had a force on the opposite or left bank of the Jumna, to co-operate with the Central India Field Force. Had the Brigade gone to Banda it would have answered a *ruse* of Sir Hugh Rose's, which was to mislead the enemy, and allow him to join Colonel Maxwell at a fordable point of the Jumna, and so open communication between Bombay and Hindostan Proper, as well as gain a reinforcement of ammunition for the now lightened tumbrils. At the time the sowar brought the dispatch, the heat was terrific, little under 100° F. at sun-rise, and the most casual observation of the European faces would have shown they were already exhausted by their morning's march. The Brigade Major rode down the column, and asked the officers of Infantry Regiments if their men were too tired to march another stage. There was not a dissenting voice, though what the men felt was another matter. Gallant fellows! not one among them but would have marched until death if ordered, and many did so. All they cared for was, to be led on from victory to victory: what could a soldier desire more? But this march was the one grand misfortune of the campaign. The faces of the men grew paler and paler, finally livid and anxious: they lost the bronzed colour they wore some ten days before, and first one, then two or three, then dozens and scores, fell out of the line of march, exhausted, dying, and dead, on the road side:

there was no water to be had, no shade, and consequently no means of restoring them. The carriage for the sick was already crammed, and the wretched bearers themselves unable to carry the palanquins ; the whole of the Staff was sick from the ardent heat ; and to crown the whole the road was lost, and near mid-day we saw in the distant mirage the tents of the 1st Brigade, looking like huge woolpacks in a lake of water. In short, we had gone to Succalee instead of Banda.

Once on that march we came to a well, and near this the whole of the 71st Highlanders fell out, and came in as they were able during the evening. When the column had arrived within a mile of the encamping ground, it crossed a dried-up stream ; where the men obtained a little dirty water by digging holes in the gravelly bed. At length the Force gained the village, but not a drop of water was found in the well there : some few wretched villagers had stored up a supply in chatties, which was seized and drunk, and officers rode in every direction to discover more. This was at length found in a deep well, round which the Force encamped : sentries were placed over it to preserve order. It was only a hardy few who had been accustomed to the sun who were not totally prostrated by that day's work, and the sick list must have been an alarming one. We could scarce get forage for our horses. The aspect of things altogether at this crisis must have caused the Major-General some considerable anxiety, knowing as he did, from spies, and reconnaisances made by Major Gall, how strongly the enemy was entrenched on our left, and how great were their numbers.

On the 13th, the 1st Brigade, which was about two miles from us on our right, again left us, and marched to Etora. Our sick compelled us to halt until the morrow, when Lieutenant-Colonel Campbell assumed command of the Brigade in place of Colonel Stewart, of H. M.'s 14th Light Dragoons, and we marched unmolested to Etora : the sick carriage of the 1st Brigade came back and helped us in. We were delayed in finding the road at starting, and by one of the large mortars, which, like the soldiery, became unstrung. The two Brigades having joined, the supply of water was no better, or more plentiful : the squabbling at the little round wells was frightful.

At three A. M. on the 15th, the Major-General with his Brigade, and Major Orr with the Hyderabad subsidiary force, again left us, and marched on the small village of Golowlee, which is situated about six miles from Calpee, and about one from the river bank. This place was reached without much difficulty : the rear guard of the Brigade was attacked by the enemy's Cavalry, with, I believe, a few casualties to the 25th Regiment ; but Major Orr forced the enemy to retreat, and encamped opposite the village of Teree, close to the left flank of the Major-General's Brigade. The enemy must have now seen himself entirely outwitted and outflanked : all the great defences he had erected on the main road were turned and useless. On seeing them subsequently, they were found to consist of deep trenches cut through the hard road, breast-works on the flanks thrown up for musketry, and batteries of heavy ordnance placed behind the trenches ; the positions were well chosen, and points selected amongst the ravines so plentiful there that left but the one road open to us. Marks of elephants and horses having been picketed hard by were visible, their tents all standing, with some few articles of clothing and food. Our passage here would have been attended with severe loss to us, had it been attempted, whereas, now the Force in part was resting on the river bank, communication was opened across the river by a pontoon bridge. No boats were visible at this point, so it was concluded the enemy had taken possession of them : the river just here was not so deep but that even a horse could ford it.

CHAPTER VIII.

ATTACK ON OUR REAR GUARD NEAR CALPEE—ACTIONS OF DIAPOORA AND MUTTRA—BATTLE OF GOLOWLEE—THE RIVER JUMNA—CAPTURE OF CALPEE—PURSUIT OF THE ENEMY—INSIDE THE TOWN AND ARSENAL—PREPARATIONS TO BREAK UP THE FORCE.

THE 2nd Brigade, left at Etora, marched at three A. M. on the 16th. It did not get clear of the village in its front until daybreak, when it proceeded to join the two forces ahead of us, but had scarcely gone three miles before the enemy could be seen in great strength on the left flank, as if they wished to investigate our long line of baggage. The Brigade halted therefore to allow it to close up, but no one who has not seen an Indian army moving can picture the difficulty attendant on keeping together the long line of animals and carts of the rudest description. I cannot say I saw any constructed without wheels, though many of them had lost them by accident: and to add to their deficiency in mechanical construction the moving power consisted of two emaciated and thirsting bullocks, and a driver, ticketed on tin 2-B. C.I.F.F., in mortal dread of his life passing over a road intersected with ravines practicable but at one point, and at that point blocked up with broken vehicles. This perhaps will give a faint idea of the time required to get along a string of four or five miles in length of such baggage. Besides this, there were thousands of bullocks laden with gram and flour, and thousands carrying ammunition, two of our eight-inch shells being a bullock's load. After halting an hour it all came within sight of the high ground, which we occupied, and our Brigade encamped on the left of Major Orr's Force, and opposite the small village of Diapoora.

The troops had scarcely breakfasted, when heavy firing was heard in the direction of our rear guard, which, on this particular occasion, was much stronger than usual, and commanded by Major Forbes, 3rd Bombay Cavalry, who had with him 170 of his own corps, a weak troop of

H. M.'s 14th Dragoons, under Lieut. Beamish, two guns R. A., 200 Irregular Horse, a company of the 3rd Bombay Europeans, one of Bombay Sappers, and 116 of the Bombay 24th N. I., under Lieut. Estridge. Arrived at the worst point in the road, which was choked up by broken and overladen hackeries, Major Forbes first saw the enemy, who had occupied Etora, the village we had just left. The approach from Calpee to this village was so thoroughly intersected with ravines, that the enormous force advancing could be only seen partially at any one time, as they came over the crests of the ridges among the ravines. In the village they commenced their attack on some unprotected hackery-drivers, killing them, and looting the carts. The drivers had managed to mistake the road in getting out of the village, and so got behind the rear guard: many of them belonged to the Commissariat Department, other lost baggage belonged to officers, and one who had invested heavily in prize property at the Jhansi sales lost it all, and perhaps the Ranee received some of her gold chains again. The number of the enemy which assailed the rear was about 6000 men, and chiefly horse: they had guns of heavy metal with them, drawn by elephants. The cavalry were dressed in the uniform of the several regiments that had mutinied. More conspiuous than all, perhaps, were those dressed in red, and those in light grey: some were in green Ulkhalucks, and a few in yellow. Their artillery fire was good, and when within about two miles and a half of camp they brought their guns up to a range of six hundred yards, and their infantry so sheltered by ravines poured in volleys: one round shot killed four of the 24th N. I., another two of the 3rd Bombay troopers, an artilleryman had his pouch shot off his belt, and a dragoon his turban shot off—he resumed it with the greatest nonchalance: in fact, the same spirit pervaded all under Major Forbes's command. His position was most critical—the slightest unsteadiness on the part of the rear guard would have furnished the little encouragement that was wanting to the enemy's cavalry to bring them on at the charge. Once or twice, indeed, they made faint attempts to come on—a small quantity more *ganja*, and it is difficult to see what the result to us would have been: as it was, though all were suffering from a parching thirst, and unable to leave the column to procure water,

Major Forbes brought them into camp intact. It was one of the most masterly feats in the campaign, and as such gained the Major-General's unqualified approbation.

The heavy cannonading and rolls of musketry fire, attending this gallant repulse of an enemy in overpowering numbers, caused our Brigadier, Colonel Campbell, to take immediate possession of the village in our right front (Muttra), and the Major-General, with almost the whole of the 1st Brigade, came down to the rescue. The enemy also seemed to be receiving reinforcements, and commenced an attack on the villages held by Colonel Campbell and Captain Hare. The 2nd Brigade derived its supply of water from near these villages, which probably induced the enemy to try and drive us out of them.

As the day wore, the action became general in our entire front, from Diapoora to the Jumna. It was so close to our tents, that had they gained any advantage we should have been driven into camp; as it was, the round shot rolled through the lines. Our men were falling out by hundreds, from exhaustion and sun-stroke; and there was one continued column of dhoolies carrying them into camp. The enemy must have suffered from the sun considerably, though not in the proportion of the natives of our force, who were exhausted and badly fed. The rebels invariably carried away their wounded and dead. It was nearly dark when the firing ceased. The enemy seemed well nigh tired as ourselves, and left us once more in quiet. We rode our own chargers to the well more than a mile in our rear, fearing to trust them to syces, as the enemy's cavalry was always watchful, and intent on capturing animals separated from the camp, and often murdered our followers. The 2nd Brigade was nearly or quite six miles from the Jumna, and we envied those in the Major-General's camp, which rested on the river bank, or as near as practicable, the ground being broken up and unfit for encamping close to the stream.

On the 17th, a mortar battery was thrown up in front of the 86th lines of the 1st Brigade, to shell the ravines towards Calpee. There was a small plain there on which the enemy's sentries were always visible, but out of rifle range. The day following nothing occurred until about 3 P. M., when all of us in the 2nd Brigade were again turned out to our left front, as the enemy had come on again in great numbers, and seemed to wish to get into our left rear. They were strong in artillery, and had two eighteen-pounder English guns; but they were soon silenced, and made to retreat, by Captain Field's battery. A singular circumstance occurred on the day of the attack on the rear guard, and was observed by the bombadiers of these guns. The enemy returned one of our nine-pounder shot, which was picked up, and again fired at the enemy; a second time it was returned at our column, and again fired at the enemy; this occurred a third time: the shot having a peculiar mark on it was distinguishable. So soon as we had driven the enemy back, they assailed the village of Muttra again, and the round shot rolled among the tents of the 14th Dragoons, causing much alarm to the followers in camp. It was not until dusk that the enemy ceased their attack. As the force in the village had been much strengthened, they had little chance of taking it from us. The 71st Highlanders, 24th N. I., and Bombay Artillery, held it, while the 14th Dragoons and Nizam's Horse, under Major Orr, kept the plain in front of it clear. This was the third day of fighting and exposure the 2nd Brigade was called on to endure; besides which, being on the extreme left of the line, it was constantly harassed by the enemy's horse, and the chief well, about a mile in our rear, had become exhausted. The little water we procured was a muddy mixture, our baggage animals began to die in great numbers, the enemy had carried off hundreds more when out foraging, and we heard with no great composure that the Commissariat Officer had not carriage enough to transport the Brigade to any other spot. That same night, too, considerable alarm was caused A report was spread that the enemy had turned our flank. Luckily it turned out entirely false; but it served to keep up the tension point to which we were all strung at that time. And the number of officers on the sick list made the duties fall very heavy on those who could work. This day's fight was chiefly an artillery one, and we lost very few in action, the sun, as on previous days, making by far the greater havoc.

On the morning of the 18th, the heavy firing of the mortar battery in front of Golowlee was heard throughout the day, and we sent to Cawnpore for doctors and bheesties.

On the 19th, the *reveille* sounded at 3 A. M., and at daybreak we were rejoiced to find we too were to encamp on the Jumna. Major Orr with his Force preceded us: the Cavalry remained to see the baggage off the ground. There was not quite sufficient carriage—a load of the Highlanders' tents remained behind, and the officer commanding the Cavalry, rather than expose his men longer to the sun, disposed of them. The enemy came out again and watched us depart, but did not attack. I believe they thought we found Calpee a trifle too strong for us, and intended to retreat across the Jumna. Our postal communication from Bombay was cut off just now, and we sent letters across the river. All our camps now rested on the right bank, one in rear of the other, with Golowlee in our front, and in advance of all a mortar battery, with a strong body of Infantry: still, it was well nigh a mile of ravines between us and the river bed. The soil was mud and calcareous conglomerate, which caused most powerful radiation of the heat, and among the ravines the hot air could not circulate, so that the journey down to the water was most oppressive and toilsome. But the sight of the calm blue sheet was inexpressibly refreshing : in fact, one could scarcely realise so much of the limpid element being at one's entire disposal, and began to question whether the mirage was not playing tricks again with one's imagination. The animals belonging to our camps wandered down in herds, and many had reached the water bnt to die. My thermometer read 115° Fahr. in a double-roofed hill tent.

At three A. M. on the morning of the 20th, Sir Hugh Rose crossed the river to direct Colonel Maxwell's attack on the city and fort, as well as the river bank intervening between our advanced picket and Calpee. There was a village on this tract about half way, which was occupied in great force by the enemy, and would of course interfere with our advance on the city, and could be easily shelled from the opposite bank. About one o'clock the enemy advanced on our mortar battery. Brigadier Stuart sent reinforcements of Infantry from the 86th and 25th Regiments: also some companies of the 24th N. I. from the 2nd Brigade. The enemy were soon driven back : ten men on our side were wounded, and about thirty struck down by the sun. Lieutenant Jerome, 86th Regiment, was struck on the forehead by a ball which I calculated must have come a distance of eight hundred yards, and therefore inferred there were rifles in the hands of the enemy. Lieutenant Forbes, 26th Regiment, and Lieutenant Estridge, 24th Regiment, both had attacks of sun-stroke. At dusk we left the mortar battery with its ordinary guard of 3rd Europeans and 86th Infantry: there were some field guns there also.

On the morning of the 21st we found reinforcements in our camp, which had crossed over to us from Maxwell's Brigade during the night. They consisted of two companies H. M.'s 88th Regt., some Riflemen mounted on camels, with Sikh drivers, and two companies of Sikh Infantry—fine soldier-like looking fellows, and sensibly dressed, not imprisoned in British uniform. It was reported that eight men of the 88th who came over received sun-strokes before 9 A. M. Indeed, the sun in early morning felt more sickening than at midday: and on the previous day, out of a foraging party of thirty-three dragoons which left camp, but nineteen returned on the saddle. The whole force was suffering in this alarming proportion, and the enemy knew this well. It was said they had spies in the camp, wearing the tin tickets they had taken from our followers killed during the attack on the rear guard; but if they had their spies, we we reeven with them, and the Major-General had gained the very correct intelligence that on the morrow we should be attacked in great force, the rebels having sworn on the sacred waters of the Jumna that they would drive us into them, and annihilate us, and, if unsuccessful, they would retreat on the Jaloun road. We were prepared for them.

At eight A. M. on the 22d, Brigadier Stuart posted himself at the mortar battery in front of our camps, taking with him half Woolcombe's battery, and some men of the 3rd European Regt. On his right, and extended as a line of skirmishers reaching along the ravines to the river, was the gallant corps of Country Downs, under Colonel Lowth; on the left of the Brigadier was a wing of the 25th N. I.; in rear and in support was a troop of H. M.'s 14th Dragoons, and one of the 3rd B. L. C. Towards the centre of our line was Colonel Robertson, with the other wing of his corps, the 25th, the remaining half of the 4th Company 2nd Battalion Bombay Artillery, under Lieutenant Strutt, and also the 21st Company Royal Engineers. On the left centre Lightfoot's troop of Horse Artillery and two troops of H. M.'s 14th, our heavy guns, and the Royal field battery, together with the 71st Highlanders and 3rd Europeans. On the extreme left was the Hyderabad Contingent force, Maxwell's Camel Riflemen and Sikhs; and as the ground at this point was more open and adapted for Cavalry, the 14th Dragoons under Colonel Gall, and 3rd Hyderabad Cavalry under Captain Abbott, occupied the front of the siege guns.

The enemy appeared a little before 9 A. M., advancing from Calpee in front of our position, certain of victory. Our videttes began to fire and fall back, but so numerous were the ravines that half the approaching force came on without being visible to us. Their Cavalry and Artillery were on the right of their line, the ravines being impracticable on the left. Our Infantry advanced, and the heavy guns opened; the ravines became filled with clouds of smoke, and the heat, increased by the excitement, was more killing than the fire of the enemy, who had discovered the weak point in our line, viz., the mortar battery, where there was a mere handful of Infantry and no supports, and the few there had been considerably lessened by sun-stroke. At this point, maddened and infuriated by narcotics and stimulants, they came on *a la Zouave*, and with about as much permanent advantage as such unstable soldiery would always gain against Englishmen. They had almost gained the mortars, when the Brigadier, Ensign Trueman, and Serjeant-Major Graham, called on the gunners to fight for their guns, which at that time were in danger : another moment, and the tide of the enemy would have rolled through our line, had not Sir Hugh Rose made one of those brilliant charges for which he is so celebrated. In this instance, at the head of the Rifle brigade on their camels, he swept down the side of the ravine in front of the mortar battery. Our right and the enemy's left were now in contact, and they broke and fled amid the cheers of the gallant Rifle corps: their masses became more and more scattered and loose, as they received the deadly volleys of grape and musketry poured into them. All now joined in the pursuit, which was carried on as long as it was judicious to allow the gallant band, so exhausted by the heat, to continue their exertions: the ravines were covered, not by our killed and wounded, but by our sun-stricken. The devotion shown by the Medical Staff must have forced itself on the notice of every one: no matter what the occasion, they were always at their post and ever in the front. Had a lesser genius commanded on that occasion, where the physical and mental energies of all were fairly exhausted by climate and watching, the Central India Field Force would, in all probability, as the rebel army had prophesied, have fled across the Jumna. There were no vast gleaming squadrons and battalions wherewith to drive back the fanatic and infuriated hordes of women murderers, but a thin red line of exhausted but daring men, who had "marched a thousand miles and taken upward of a hundred guns," badly fed and footsore, galled and weighed down by ill-contrived uniform, and fighting in a medium of 130° or 140° of heat, thirsting for water.

It is impossible to record the numerous individual acts of gallantry displayed that day, when but one spirit animated the whole line—how the Brigadier prepared to die at his guns rather than yield an inch—how the natives of the force withstood the taunts and gibes hurled at them by their own kith and kin for their adherence to the British cause ; but half this credit may be fairly given to their officers and Commandant, Colonel Robertson. Captain Lightfoot and Lieutenant Strutt shed lustre on the Bombay Artillery ; and the casualties among the horses ridden by the Staff showed they had not spared themselves.

This day's work did more to undeceive the conceit which had been planted in the bosoms of the sepoys of Bengal than twenty years' change of system would have worked, were it ever so perfect. Every imaginable cause was in their favour, and their day's valour, purchased at the price of the next day's prostration, from the effects of opium and bhang, availed them nothing. Maxwell's Force on the opposite bank had placed their artillery in position, and during the flight of the sepoys on Calpee opened across the stream with the best effect. The shells could be seen bursting over the half-way village, as well as in the fort and town of Calpee itself.

The advantage of so signal a success was not to be lost, and it was rumoured we were to advance on Calpee itself on the following day. No orders, however, appeared until 10 P. M. in the evening (Sunday), when all troops were directed to take a day's provisions cooked ready for use. The Cavalry and Artillery were to leave at 3 A. M. on the following morning, taking the Calpee road towards Jaloun; the Infantry were to march up the river bank, taking with them the Cavalry baggage; the remainder, including the 2nd Brigade, Artillery park, Bazar, and Commissariat stores, hospitals and sick, to assemble in front of Golowlee, and be guarded by a small force under Captain Hare, consisting of a troop of 3rd Bombay Light Cavalry, some Hyderabad Cavalry and Infantry, with four guns, and four companies 24th B. N. I. All was now ready for a general advance on the city and arsenal by daybreak. Colonel Maxwell continued to shell the approaches, as well as the half-way village (Rehree), until the advance was made, and his riflemen, who were stationed on the bank immediately opposite Calpee, annoyed the rebel sepoys considerably when they descended the river bank for water. The whole of the ferry-boats were in their possession, and fastened beneath the city.

The enemy having lost heart completely, made the advance on Calpee town and fort, which took place on the 23rd, an almost bloodless affair. The troops fell in, the Infantry forming one long line, with Cavalry and Artillery some distance in the rear as reserves. The 86th Regiment taking the ground of yesterday, under their Colonel, swept the ravines down to the river. The centre of the line was under the immediate command of Brigadier Stuart, and its left under Colonel Campbell, of the 71st Highlanders. Sir Hugh Rose, with the 2nd column, including the Hyderabad contingent troops, also advanced, but considerably to the westward, moving along the Calpee road. Both started about 3 A. M.: Colonel Gall and Captain Abott, with the Cavalry, as well as the mounted Riflemen, accompanied the Major-General. The columns, in advancing through the ravines as beaters do when driving out game, started a panther and two hares: all were killed by the Highlanders. No opposition, or scarcely any, was made until the line arrived at the half-way village, Rehree, which, notwithstanding the shells which came across the Jumna, was occupied by rebel infantry, who fired a few rounds, and fled before the Royal County Downs, who fired the village. The line again advanced until it came in sight of dense crowds of the enemy, which appeared to be in readiness to fight, but at the same time were moving off with their guns and baggage. The general's column also met with small resistance: one battery opened, but quickly retreated after a few rounds from our guns, and we could see the main body of the enemy making a rapid retreat also. An order was sent to the 1st column, under Brigadier Stuart, to continue his advance on the city. Seeing our troops come on, the enemy fled, and the Cavalry, under Colonel Gall, started in pursuit. The Infantry gained the city and fort without the slightest resistance: the enemy had left it to a man, and some large buildings, which had apparently been built for pressing and storing cotton, afforded grateful shelter to the troops during the heat of the day.

The Cavalry and Horse Artillery were more fortunate than to be able to enjoy ease. Led by Major Gall, five weak troops of Dragoons, and Lightfoot's battery, together with the 3rd Regiment of Hyderabad Cavalry under Captain

Abbott, they followed the Jaloun road, where the rebels still occupied some temples, but vacated them in disorder as we approached. A short gallop, and the Dragoons and dusky *Sabreurs* of the Contingent were among the now terrified fugitives. Some fought, others were too much taken up with their flight to resist. The sight of our Cavalry appalled them, and three hundred were slain, six guns captured, with their paraphernalia and ammunition, together with six elephants, eight camels, forty bullocks, and some wheeled vehicles. Captain Lightfoot with his guns disorganised a mass of about five hundred men, and Captain Need with his troop cut up two hundred of them, Lieutenants Giles and Beamish making great havoc with their revolvers, and Captain Abbott taking a nine-pounder English gun. There were women among the fugitives, who are said to have fired on their pursuers. This was by far the most complete rout of the campaign. The ground was covered by an endless number and variety of arms, and in the abandoned baggage carts were English officers' uniforms, and a vast quantity of French grey cloth, such as was used in making the clothing of the Bengal Cavalry.

Judging from a collection of buttons made from the dead bodies, parts of eleven Bengal and Gwalior Infantry corps were engaged. The men in charge of the guns cut the traces, sprang on the backs of the horses which had been harnessed to them, and rode for their lives. The heat of the day being so excessive, and the horses as well as men suffering from thirst, not more than forty of our Cavalry were in at the finish, and the enemy's Cavalry, who had so cruelly abandoned their brethren on foot, seeing this, began to form up in considerable strength, and the pursuit was necessarily abandoned. Lightfoot's horses could go no further. The column now returned to camp, which had been pitched about 5 P. M. in frònt of Calpee.

During the day our gallant General, again almost beaten by the sun, would not return to camp, but sought the shelter of a tree to recover sufficiently to proceed with his anxious work. The men, too, who had been in the pursuit swelled up the list of sick. Two men, with camels belonging to Captain Abbott, who had been seized by the enemy while out foraging some days before, took advantage of the confusion prevailing during their flight and escaped, returning to our camp. They bore marks of severe flagellation, and had been closely examined about our strength, &c. They informed us, that many men had left after their defeat on the day previous to our advance on the place, and that the Ranee of Jhansi and Nawab of Banda had gone at 12 o'clock that same night. They further stated, that the Ranee's departure was somewhat hastened by one of the shells from Maxwell's force bursting in her room, and killing two attendants. The camels were safely brought back with their loads of the rebel property, consisting chiefly of tentage, sepoys' coats, a chair, and some clothing.

Captain Hare, with his Regiment of Hyderabad Infantry, was placed in charge of the fort, and the brigade encamped near the "Eighty tombs." The ground was full of ravines, and hillocks covered with sharp cutting sand, which, carried by the hot wind, became exceedingly annoying and painful to the eyes, but we no longer suffered from want of water. On entering the town, which is on the right bank of the Jumna, the channel of which just here is a mile and a half wide (though, as it was the dry season, the water flowed under the right bank, leaving a mile of heavy sand on the opposite side of the bed) we found the streets and outskirts traversed by rugged ravines, and built of the conglomerate of which the high river bank is composed. The fort scarcely deserves such a dignified appellation, being simply a fortified square situated on the margin of the precipitous river bank, fifty feet above the level of the stream. An 18-pounder would breach it in a few hours, but the approach to it would be difficult on account of the very deep and numerous ravines. Out of a population of nearly 30,000, scarcely a creature could be seen in the streets, Tantia Topee having given out, some days previously, that all those who valued their lives had better leave. The dead and decomposing bodies of men killed by Maxwell's mortars, placed in a dry jheel opposite, were now matters of contention between the pigs and pariah dogs, with which the place appeared infested. The houses had been knocked about considerably by shells, and the enemy had cut all the trees down at the root, and destroyed one European bungalow near the river, which had apparently been a very handsome one. Some smaller houses of European construction, probably occupied by men in charge of the arsenal, were also in ruins. There was little or no loot found in the town: the fort, and its munitions of war in such vast quantities, was the prize. The entry to it was along a small drawbridge which crossed a dry moat, and subsequently through a slightly tortuous passage. Almost the whole of the inside was covered by tents, shamiahnas, palls, and routees, under which the greater part of the garrison had lived. Sepoy uniform and arms were scattered over the floors of all of them. There was an indescribable medley here, just as in the fort of Jhansi, but the articles here all pertained to the art of war. There were guns, large and small, numbering fifteen, besides a large mortar and howitzer: there were conical stacks of English round shot and shell, and several sheds in which the manufacture of cannon, howitzers, shells, and the repair of arms, was being carried on. The tools and appliances, such as forges, hammers, vices, smith's braces, &c., were all of English make. Several muskets had been re-stocked, and very well fitted. There were vast numbers of broken brass shells, which proved they had rather failed in that branch of ordnance manufacture:

they had all been cast on clay moulds, and the outside filed smooth. In the arsenal the uniform was knee deep, comprising not only sepoy clothes, but coats that had been taken from Windham's slain, belonging to H. M.'s 88th Regiment, some bearing the number 92, with the Prince of Wales' plume; also one or two ladies' bonnets, together with brass-band instruments, parts of cornopeans, French horns, trumpets, and Infantry bugles, Military drums, flags, standards, Glengarries, stocks, caps, pouches, belts, and boxes of musket cartridges. Underground, and discovered subsequently, was a vast store of ammunition, including 60,000 pounds of English gunpowder, shot, shell, and fire arms. In fact, this was the great central arsenal of the mutineers, and had it been capable of defence it would not have fallen such an easy prey to us. They had no gallant spirit of the Willoughby mould among them, or the match would have been applied, converting the whole into a mass of debris, to have been borne away by the deep blue waters of the soft-flowing Jumna. There was a vast pile of well-made cylinders of red pottery, closed at one end, and partially so at the other: no one knew or could venture to guess their use, but they were particularly useful as coojas to cool water. It was thought by some they were to throw inflammable material on assailing parties. The view from the high bank on which the fort stood was extensive, and the winding river gave it a refreshing tone. The flat-bottomed cotton boats were all found fastened beneath the bank, and Maxwell's camp could be seen in the distance, in the direction of Cawnpore.

On the same evening of the day on which we became masters of Calpee, Lieut.-Colonel Robertson, with his corps the 25th N. I., proceeded on the rebel track, and on the following morning a troop of Dragoons, with a squadron of 3rd Bombay Cavalry, 150 Hyderabad Sowars, and No. 18 Field Battery, commanded by Lieut. Harcourt, also followed to join the 25th Regiment, thus forming a column of observation. But as all accounts agreed the rebels would cross the Jumna, and make toward Delhi, their fate became a matter of bygone interest. We heard, too, of a Bengal force guarding the ford on the river where it was expected they would pass over, and to this force we in camp consigned them, and enjoyed the comparative rest which apparently awaited us. The European wounded and sick, together with a great number of sick officers, went to Cawnpore, distant thirty-five miles, and it was rumoured in camp the Central India Field Force would break up, and the General proceed to Poona *viâ* Cawnpore and Calcutta, while the troops would be distributed between Gwalior, Calpee, and Jhansi.

On the morning of the 29th a further reinforcement went out to Major Robertson's column, in the shape of a squadron of H. M.'s 14th Dragoons, and a wing of H. M.'s 86th Regiment. It appears that this column having arrived at Srawun, about 35 miles from Calpee, discovered the rebels had not taken the direction which every one supposed they would—across the Jumna ford—but had actually been reinforced by mutineers from Bareilly, and were at Indoorkee, on the Scinde river, this being part of the dominions of the Maharajah Scindiah. Even this intelligence did not awaken the suspicion that his capital was menaced, and arrangements went on for the distribution of the force. It was said Whitlock's Saugor Field division had been ordered to garrison

Calpee, but it as yet stuck fast at Banda, with a cavalry column at the Chilkatara ford on the Jumna.

At length all doubts were solved by the appearance of Sir Hugh Rose's farewell order, and the actual move towards the Dekkan of the Nizam's Contingent troops, under Major Orr, to whom the reduction of some fractious Thakoors and Zemindars on his route was entrusted: and on the morning of the 4th of June Captains Hare and Abbott left, with their corps of Infantry and Cavalry. Many officers who had been appointed to other duties took advantage of this as an escort, and, without a regret, bade adieu to the deadly banks of the sacred river. Further intelligence, received in Sir Hugh Rose's camp that same day by Sir Robert Hamilton, placed it beyond a doubt that the rebels had gone towards Gwalior, which fact looked extremely significant. An express was sent to the Hyderabad troops to halt until further orders, and Brigadier Stuart, with the 1st Brigade, was ordered to march rapidly to reinforce Lieutenant-Colonel Robertson.

CHAPTER IX.

REVOLT OF THE MAHARAJAH SCINDIAH'S ARMY—ADVANCE OF OUR TROOPS ON GWALIOR—ACTION AT MORAR—WE ENTER THE CANTONMENTS—ACTION AT KOTAH-KE-SERAI—DEATH OF THE RANEE—THE CAPTURE OF THE "TWO CITIES"—ROSE IS MORTALLY WOUNDED IN TAKING THE FORT—BATTLE OF JOWRA-ALIPORE—REINSTATEMENT OF THE MAHARAJAH SCINDIAH ON HIS THRONE—THE GWALIOR STAR.

ON the 5th of June the worst fears were realised by the astounding news that the capital of the Maharajah, with all his treasure and jewels, had fallen into the hands of the mutineers, and the whole of his army had gone over in a body to the rebel standard, while Scindiah himself, after going out to do battle with the rebels at Bahadurpoor, had narrowly escaped with his life by flight to Agra. Our force, worn out by the temperature, watching, and toilsome marches, could be brought to believe such unwelcome news with the greatest reluctancy.

On the 6th of June, Sir Hugh Rose himself, though worn out, ill, and proceeding on sick certificate, girded up his loins once more to be the herald of victory: and he present, though we anticipated a second enaction of the siege of Delhi, no one doubted our success. Who can predict what would have followed had the stronghold of Gwalior remained in rebel grasp even a fourth part of the time Delhi was held by its king? Huge clouds and storms, the forerunners of the rainy season, had already shown themselves, and one foresaw our gaunt and spectre force a prey to cholera, fever, and dysentery, and hoped against hope the intelligence might yet prove false.

The Major-General arrived at Attaria on the 7th of June, with a troop of Horse Artillery, two squadrons of Cavalry, and the Madras Sappers and Miners, having effected a junction with the Hyderabad troops on the road. At this place a dispatch from Lt.-Colonel Robertson not only confirmed, but gave the particulars of the revolt of Scindiah's army, from which it appeared a mock fight had been performed, in which some horses were killed, and, by a plan preconcerted by Tantia Topee, the troops of our ally had gone with their artillery into the pay and service of the aspirant to the throne of the Peshwarate, the portals of the city, fort, and arsenal of Gwalior had been thrown open, and the fabulous wealth, English munitions of war, and pieces of ordnance, were all arrayed against us. This was indeed a timely and welcome reinforcement to the enemy, while we had again been weakened by the detachment of another garrison at Calpee, which comprised a great part of the 2nd Brigade. This was, however, eventually to follow us when relieved by troops expected from Bengal. Brigadier Smith, with the Rajpootana F. F., had been ordered from Sipree to Kotah-ke-Serai east of Gwalior, and Major Orr, who had *en route* to Jhansi attacked a Thakoor with a force of 300 men, killing one third of them, was directed to retrace his steps and halt at Punniar, an old battle-field south-west fourteen miles from Gwalior. Lord Clyde had sent a force from Agra, which the Major-General directed to remain on the north side : it consisted of a field battery, a wing of Meade's Horse, a regiment of European Infantry, 200 Sikhs, with siege ordnance.

Thus with our advance from the east this stronghold was in a fair way of being invested, so far as our limited numbers allowed. Our column marched every night about 11 P. M., and we reached our encamping grounds about sun-rise. The heat, if anything, seemed to increase day by day.

On the 11th we caught up Brigadier Stuart, with the 1st Brigade, at a small fort on the Scinde river, called Indoorkee. Here the Gwalior mutiny was planned and matured. The roads hereabouts were extremely bad, cut up by water-courses and ravines occasionally, but a narrow pass existing such as one gharry would completely obstruct : once, after crossing the Patrooj river, we were delayed half the night—the bazaar, all carried on carts, had preceded us, and completely arrested our progress. The whole affair deserved, and narrowly escaped, burning by order of Sir Hugh. The misery of the drowsy pace at which we were compelled to follow our way, trammelled as we were with heavy ordnance, and worn-out draught animals, was almost the greatest trial we were called on to endure, and then to be obliged to halt about every hundred yards, and battle against sleep, was aggravating in the extreme. The Cavalry constantly slept in their saddles while marching, and by the constant lounging and dragging to one side galled their chargers' backs as they dreamt

> ...." of battle begun,
> Of field-day and foray, and foeman undone;
> Of provinces sacked, and warrior store,
> Of hurry and havoc, and hampers of ore;
> Of captive maidens for joys abundant,
> And ransom vast when these grow redundant.
> Hurrah for the foray! Fiends ride forth a-souling,
> For the dogs of havoc are yelping and yowling."

At Amyne, which was reached on the 12th, we found forage laid in store for us by Scindiah's orders, and just as we dismounted a group of officers were seated under the scanty shade afforded by some bushes of camel thorn, reading the first copy of the Jhansi dispatches which had arrived in camp, and by the kind courtesy of Sir Robert Hamilton had been lent to the listening group. Many a worse subject for transfer to canvass has graced the walls of our fine-art galleries, and the disappointment pourtrayed in some of the faces would have tried the painter's skill. It was one of the characteristics of Sir Hugh Rose to mention but few to the favorable consideration of their country and Queen, instead of following the style of the volumes of dispatches which have lately poured into the Adjutant-General's department, in most of which indiscriminate, and therefore less prized, praise has been showered on all officers engaged; and a wondrous similarity of wording, and monotony of literature, runs throughout them. I never saw that dispatch since that day. It did not contain my name, and therefore had not one molecule of interest for me. I had received my reward in being present at Jhansi. The Bengal troops had arrived to garrison Calpee, and the weakemed 2nd Brigade, which had been left behind, was only 17 miles in our rear at the village of Mahona. But one medical officer remained with it, and he was sun-stricken, and the men of the 3rd Europeans were in a most distressing state. An unlucky Assistant-Surgeon was ordered back the weary seventeen miles of enemy's country, without even an orderly as a guard. * * *

About this time Brigadier-General Napier, K.C.B., arrived, and assumed command of the 2nd Brigade; and on the 16th June we arrived in sight of Gwalior. Intervening between the fortress and our force were the English cantonments, embosomed in bright green trees, with a picturesque church steeple and bungalow roofs peeping out from among them. They were as familiar faces, and associated strangely with the rebel ranks drawn up in front of them. They were a loadstone which drew us on them one day sooner than the will of our General dictated, for we had come a long night's march, and lacked the energy to fight. Once again Englishmen were called on to be up and doing, while the igneous-born rock of Gwalior looked on.

The two Brigades, having assumed the order of battle—the 1st and 1st line being under the immediate command of Sir Hugh, and the 2nd, which was exceedingly weak, numbering about a thousand men, under General Napier, C.B. —steadily advanced against the enemy in front of the cantonments. scaring, as they passed, the birds of prey which were gorging themselves on the dead horses left by Scindiah's troops, when pretending to oppose the advance of the rebels on his capital. As we advanced, the enemy retired under cover of the cantonment houses and trees. Our baggage came in our rear, and was protected by the second line, which advanced *en echelon* from the right. The enemy commenced the fire by opening on this line from a powerful battery. The whole of our Artillery was with the 1st Brigade, and replied in a manner which soon rendered inert the rebel guns, and with a strong line of skirmishers belonging to H. M.'s 86th, 71st, 25th Native Infantry, Madras Sappers, and Hyderabad Infantry, we marched rapidly into the cantonments, driving the rebels before us. This valuable point was not gained, however, without considerable loss or difficulties. The ground to our left was full of ravines filled by the fresh troops of the Maharajah, and it was in driving them out that the 71st Highlanders lost an Officer, Lieutenant Neave, and five or six men, besides other casualties happening from wounds. They had almost arrived within musket length of the rebels, when young Neave fell, shot through the breast, and while the sepoy was reloading, and exulting over the deed, he fell, riddled by rifle bullets : in fact, every inch of this irregular ground was taken in dispute. On the enemy's left, too, the ground was treacherous, and sadly hampered and impeded our Cavalry, among which, especially in the

3rd Hyderabad Contingent Regiment, were many casualties. The County Downs now swept through the main street of Morar, and Captain Abbott led his Regiment in pursuit, which turned them on the plain, where a squadron of H. M.'s 14th Dragoons swooped down upon them, and swelled the number of their slain. Another troop of this Regiment, with the 2nd Brigade, led by Lieutenant Gowan, charged the rebels as they fled from the ravines, and cut up some five and twenty men. In two hours we had won for ourselves the invaluable shelter of Morar. It was not a place the enemy would have sacrificed much to hold, being incapable of being converted into a strong position; but had their flight been less precipitate they would, beyond a doubt, have destroyed the temporary sheds and provisions Scindiah had stored for us, expecting, as he did, a part of the Central India Field Force would pass the rainy season there. We were now within five miles of the city and fort, and the shade afforded by the two long avenues running the entire length of Morar was most grateful: several houses had been repaired, and long sheds built, which served as hospitals for the sick, whilst others served the purpose of

Commissariat and Ordnance stores. A comfortable residence had been prepared for the Brigadier, built in a style half English, half Oriental, reminding one of the stucco villas in the suburbs of Bath or Cheltenham. The Church, too, was in tolerable preservation, save its minarets and interior furniture, which had been destroyed. We pitched our tents on what were formerly the well-cared-for gardens of the officers of the Contingent, and which were still covered by flowers and shrubs, lime, custard apple, and pomegranate trees, and vines.

On the day following the one on which we entered the cantonments, Brigadier Smith, commanding a Brigade of the Rajpootana Field Force, arrived at Kotah-ke-Serai, which is situated four miles S. E. of Gwalior; and while preparing to encamp, numbers of the enemy appeared coming on to attack him. They were in hilly and broken ground, which caused the Brigadier to withdraw his force into more open plain in the rear: at the same time his baggage was placed near the fort existing there. The enemy's line advanced and gave battle, opening a heavy artillery fire. The Horse Artillery galloped to the front, driving the enemy to the hilly ground. H. M.'s 95th Regiment, led by Colonel Raines, advanced in skirmishing order, supported by the 10th Regiment Bombay N. I. under Colonel Pelly. The impetuous manner in which these fine corps did their work caused the rebels to disappear from behind their breast-works, which were taken by a charge, and the pursuit continued to the summit of an opposite and distant ridge ; but on ascending this, the enemy were discovered with guns in position, together with crowds of Cavalry and Infantry : the round shot and shell from these checked further advance. The enemy now brought guns to infilade the 95th and 10th Regiments, but these were also silenced by Bombay Artillery. Colonel Raines led the Infantry on the Gwalior road with intend to attack the scarlet Cavalry of Gwalior, but they retired steadily on to the plain of Phool Bagh, and subsequently in hovering round, awaiting the courage to charge, they received a regular volley from the 95th, wich left vacancies in their ranks. The heights about the plain being occupied by us, and the pass leading to it also held by us, a Squadron of H. M.'s 8th Hussars rehearsed one of those charges originally performed at Balaklava, dashing from the mouth of the pass, sweeping down the enemy, never drawing rein, until they had gone completely through the enemy's camp in the Phool Bagh, a distance of nearly two miles. The men, though young soldiers, proved they had been cast in the same mould as those who fell at Balaklava. They slew great numbers, and took two guns besides possessing themselves of the greater part of the camp equipage. The intense excitement, added to the temperature, produced the worst effects on the men, who returned in a terrible state of exhaustion; and of their three gallant leaders, Colonel Hicks, Captains Heneage and Morris, one, Captain Heneage, with difficulty recovered. The use the Hussars made in this charge of their very efficient breech-loading carbines, was pleasurable to see—the killed were upwards of two hundred rebels. Memorable too for another reason is this affair: the gallant Queen of Jhansi fell from a carbine wound, and was carried to the rear, where she expired, and was burnt according to the custom of Hindoos. Thus the brave woman cemented with her blood the cause she espoused. It is as well it was so, and that she did not survive to share the ignominious fate of Tantia Topee. The fact of her death was not known to us for some days, as she was attired as a Cavalry soldier. Even the report was received with doubt, untill Sir Robert Hamilton established it irrefragably. The ardour of the Hussars led them too far for their exhausted condition : they were therefore retired, and the enemy, having recovered from the panic into which they had been thrown, rallied on all sides, whereupon our troops were withdrawn within the defile under protection of the Infantry, and the camp was pitched for the night in an amphitheatre of hills. The day's exposure, ending at 7 P. M., cost the 95th Regiment alone ninety sun-strokes, including five officers, and on the morrow eight of this large number proved fatal : the 8th Hussars also lost some men from the same cause.

The next morning (18th) the remnant of the second Brigade, which had been left behind at Calpee, marched into Morar, and no sooner had it arrived than Sir Hugh Rose marched off with the 1st Brigade, leaving the 2nd under command of General Napier in the cantonments. The sun was yet far distant from the hill tops when the troops left to skirt round the city to

Kota-ke-Serai, full twenty miles, and during the whole day we heard the report of the enemy's cannon, which were placed on a ridge to the left of Brigadier Smith's position, and threw shot into his camp. It was a most trying march, and upwards of a hundred Infantry knocked up.

At night, we slept on the banks of the Morar river, and in the morning Scindiah arrived from Agra to see the Battle of Gwalior, in preparation for which Sir Hugh Rose commenced to reconnoitre the ground and enemy's positions, and to bridge over the canal that intervened between us and the enemy's battery on the ridge. Gordon's company of Madras Sappers and Miners were set to this task, and shewed themselves as equal to that work as they were to fight. Indeed, so long as they were supplied with their dram they worked as merrily as English navvies. Some heavy guns were placed in position to silence the rebel battery on the ridge, but they were unsuccessful. One or two of our elephants, and some Artillerymen, were killed, some stacks of forage near the canal fired, and considerable reinforcements of guns and Infantry ascended the ridge, while their advanced Infantry commenced an attack on our left, which drew Her Majesty's 86th, 95th, and 10th and 25th Regiments of Infantry across the canal, where they attacked both flanks of the enemy's Infantry. The County Downs, rushing up the ridge, drove them through their own battery, taking three English guns and chasing the enemy towards Gwalior, while the men of the 95th, and 10th Bombay Regiment, turned the captured ordnance, and plied them with their own ammunition. Lieutenant Roome, leading the 10th, cleared another height occupied by the enemy, driving them down the slopes to Gwalior, and capturing five more pieces of cannon. We were now fairly before the two cities, the old situated on the eastern base of the rock, and built before the Christian era, surrounded by trees and gardens, and studded by palaces and monumental buildings, while the fort, built on the rock, was the conspicuous background, its dull frown being relieved by the citadel surmounted by kiosks. On the left of the old city was the new, a germ from the ancient Mahratta camp, which has taken good root, and is now becoming a flourishing city, furnished with barracks, magazines, parade grounds, and fine public buildings. Our line advanced on the new city, which is called the Luskar, while our camp remained in the amphitheatre of hills, well protected, and the 1st Bombay Lancers under Owen, No. 4 Bombay Battery, and a squadron of H. M.'s 14th Dragoons, ascended a plateaux formerly occupied by the enemy. This movement, together with the advance of the Infantry, caused the withdrawal of the two heavy guns which had been brought on the parade ground to bear on H. M.'s 86th Regiment. At this crisis the foresight of the Major-General pointed out to him the "Tale of the two Cities" could be told by nightfall ; and though he had proposed to delay the final advance on Gwalior until the morrow, matters had proceeded too far to delay. A rapid movement to the plain in our front ensued, the various commanding officers received their orders, the enemy were moving in all directions, and firing furiously. All was done that Generalship could accomplish : the rest could but be trusted to the pluck of British soldiers and the Fortune of War.

The word was given, and our columns, like pent-up floods suddenly released, rolled over the plain towards our adversaries. Our guns flashed out shrapnel over them, their gunners grew unsteady, turned, and fled to the shelter of the city. The Bombay Lancers swept them over their bloody track, and with a gallant but ill-directed zeal pursued them through the streets of the Luskar, which caused them the loss of one of their brave leaders. Lieutenant Mills received a mortal wound, which was rapidly avenged by his brother officer Loch, who shot the rebel in the pursuit. The Infantry, chiefly H. M.'s 95th, under Colonel Raines, and 10th Bombay, led by Lieutenat Roome, ran through the streets, but the rebels fled in the greatest confusion (their Light Horse as usual leading) in the direction of the British Residency, which is seven or eight miles from Gwalior, in the Agra direction. They were taking away a large number of guns and ammunition waggons, but Brigadier Smith, with the horsed part of his Brigade, gave pursuit, overtook, faught, and captured several guns, and only allowed the remnant to escape because the exhausted men and cattle could go no further in the darkness; for night had not closed the work. Here, as ever heretofore, did the 14th Dragoons and Bombay Horse Artillery add to their now weighty crown of laurels. At dusk on that sultry day in that sultry month did Sir Hugh Rose write himself the captor of the two cities, and placed Major Robertson in position to command them. While our troops poured through the streets, the black stronghold in the rock continued to salute us with its guns, and round shot flew through the air. This was rather singular, especially as some officials belonging to the Maharajah, who stated they had been detained as prisoners, appeared before Sir Hugh, and told him the fort was evacuated. It was closely invested through the night. Lieutenants Rose and Waller, with a party of sepoys of their Regiment, had charge of the gate, and at daylight the guns again fired on the new city. Rose and Waller led their men, and some of Scindiah's police, up the road leading to the gateway : it is long, winding, and not steep, and is terminated by a flight of very shallaw steps. The first or main gate, called Hatipul, being closed, opposed their further progress untill it was forced open, when the gallant Rose dashed in, not giving the desperate garrison time to resist him by closing the six other gates which guard the entrance : and on gaining the archway of the fortress, a gun which had been planted there failed to stay him and his men, who now closed with the rebels, a small body of fanatics and fakeers, sworn to die ; but Rose, who had escaped from Gwalior when the Contingent mutinied, and had served through the entire campaign, was sworn to die, and broke through the demon band, falling mortally wounded by the side of eight of his men. But he had taken the stupendous fortress, and died a hero's death : none during the whole campaign fell more beloved or so much regretted. And now, while standing under the shadow of this giant fort of India, we could estimate the good work done in a space of time half incredible—forged in the bowels of the earth and born of nature's womb to defy assault, its abrupt and overhanging cliffs further aided by all that man could do, crowned as it was by a parapet bristling with Artillery, entered through passages of tortuous and heavy masonry, watched by the muzzles of traversing guns, closed by seven gates, provided with tanks of water at a height of three hundred and fifty feet, and with shelter for the Garrison from the missiles of civilised warfare. Yet the hatters of our rule held it not, because they wanted a chief. Tantia they had, it is true, but he was always first to fly : his great talent lay in organising retreats, of which he was the hero until his death. Here, with all in his favour, money, troops, guns, provisions, and position, he fled while the engagement was at its hottest, weakening his force by drawing off numbers of Cavalry as a guard, and setting to his men a base and cowardly example which went unpunished till the halter encircled his Bunniah-born neck at Sipree.

The force under Brigadier General Napier, which had been left in charge of the Cantonments, having had a day's rest, started the morning after the capture of Gwalior in pursuit. After marching from seven o'clock in the morning until the sun was setting, accomplishing twenty-five miles under a terrific sun, it was reported the pursued, 10,000 strong, with many guns, were still some miles distant. It was therefore impossible to do more that night : the march had been somewhat lengthened on account of the force having been fired on while passing the Gwalior fort on its way out, thus necessitating its taking a circuitous road. After a bivouack at the village of Samowlee, until 4 A. M. on the following morning, it advanced on Jowra Alipore, where the enemy was found in force near the village, their rich park of Artillery in the centre, supported by their Infantry, while their Cavalry hovered about the flanks. They opened fire on our line, which was small enough for the occasion. Lightfoot's troop of Bombay Horse Artillery, supported by sixty of H. M.'s 14th Light Dragoons, with two hundred and fifty 3rd Regiment Hyderabad Cavalry under Abbott, were on the .right of the guns and slightly in advance, while about one hundred and fifty of the Bombay 3rd Cavalry under Lt. Dick, and a squadron of Meade's Horse, acted as a reserve. The Horse Artillery guns now galloped round a small rising ground intervening, and opened fire on the enemy's right flank. They turned and fled. The Horse Artillery gunnes and Abbott's Regiment together dashed into the enemy's battery, which was taken almost without resistance. The Cavalry commenced cutting up the fugitives, who sought the cover of villages for shelter : some three or four hundred finished their ill-starred career, and hecame food for the bald-scalped vultures and hungry jackals. The villages for six miles round about were cleared by parties of dismounted Sowars and Dragoons, in which many instances of valour were displayed, and Brigadier General Napier saw fit to ask for the Victoria Cross to reward private Nowell of the 14th K. L. D.: he in a dauntless manner pursued his victim into a village street, and under a heavy fire accounted for him. But the most gratifying scene was the twenty-six pieces of ordnance which appeared in the streets of Morar in the morning of the 26th, on the return of the pursuing column. The guns were mostly English six-pounders: twenty-five were of brass and one of iron, including two howitzers. An elephant also was taken; but Tantia Topee and the Rao Sahib had gone off on the day previous with the Gwalior treasure.

Little now remained to be done excepting the formal reinstatement of Scindiah on his throne, and a second disposition of the force. At sunrise on the 28th, Sir Hugh Rose and Staff, together with all Officers off duty, escorted the Maharajah to his palace in Phool Bagh. The streets and houses which had so recently been despoiled by his faithless soldiery were now lit up by the gay faces and many-coloured draperies of a hundred and fifty thousand of his subjects assembled to greet him on his return, each outwardly manifesting his gladness. The usual ceremonies of the Durbar were passed through, and Scindiah expressed himself very desirous to be allowed to signify, by some gift to the Central India Field Force, the great service we had done him. The gift shaped itself into a star of most elegant design, the metal to be of frosted silver, the crest of the Prince of Gwalior, a snake of gold to entwine the bar—the word "Gwalior," and figures 1858, to be engraven on a facet where the bars cross, and an orange ribbon to suspend it. A more delicately appropriate reward could not have been conceived, and as it has pleased the Major-General to recommend it, and H. R. H. the Duke of Cambridge to approve, little doubt remains but it will be given: it would be better received than a donation of Batta, and be a far more lasting memorial of the time when we warred with a double enemy, the climate and our species.

On the following day Sir Hugh Rose gave over command to Brigadier-General Napier, and regretted by all departed for a more peaceful command in the Dekkan. He is yet in the flesh to receive his reward : it is well if he does, and that it is not left for a future generation to disturb his remains that due homage be done them. Such is the custom of the present age.

The rain now fell in torrents, and brought refreshment to the dying soldiery, while it washed the blood stains from well nigh a score of our battle fields. And now Tantia with his demon horde commenced a lawless, marauding, and vagabond flight through the country, always apparently having the Dekkan in his view as the promised land ; but unfortunately for him, the man before the rustle of whose standard all rebels had learnt to quail, had preceded him, and taken authority there. Tantia and his myrmidons were allowed no rest. Sweeping like a locust cloud over districts, they left the same sad effects behind. Gradually and gradually with his Gwalior treasure his influence declined and star began to set, though occasionally and again some rebel Rajah, with a thousand robbers, would join his standard and cause his light to flicker and shine for a moment ; but his reinforcements made him more liable to be attacked, and then he became more obscure than before. The Bombay Government, by means of the Bullock Train running some six hundred miles, were enabled to send up constant reinforcements of troops and supplies of stores, and notwithstanding it was the rainy season, and even the Agra Trunk road axle deep in black mud, it covered the country with flying forces—and fly they did, over mountain, dale, and river, over districts without roads, and where Europeans had scarce or never been before, in pursuit of the Will-o'the-Wisp Tantia. He would only fight when escape was unavoidable, and then invariably was beaten and lost his guns, but never lost heart. He made for the nearest Rajah, and by force or threat replaced them, and replenished his coffers; and in proportion as the chiefs of Native States were favourable to our rule, insomuch did they suffer.

CHAPTER X.

PURSUIT OF TANTIA—A HALT AT KOTAH—BUNGALOW AND GRAVE OF THE BURTONS—THE RAJAH'S ARMY—THE RAJAH—HIS PALACE—THE NAUTCH—ELEPHANT FIGHT—SACRED FISH—PRESERVED HOG—AN ACCOMMODATING TIGER.

THERE were Divisions, Brigades, Regiments and Detachments of Troops, Regular and Irregular, commanded by officers of all ranks, the heavier the force the slower the pace, and therefore less chance of catching the swift-footed rebel chief, who carried no tents, no provisions; these he looted as he wanted them for consumption, and when his horses were worn out, left them on the road to die, and replaced them after the same manner, sometimes from our post stations, and sometimes by attacking our long lines of baggage and led horses. His Light

Horse could hover round us like shadows, and always get away from our overworked Irregular or overweighted Regular Cavalry. Each fresh Commandant who took the field fancied he could catch Tantia: prodigious marches were made, officers and men threw aside all baggage, even their tents, and accomplished upwards of forty miles daily—the rebels did fifty. The end was, our horses were all sore-backed, and the halt of a week or ten days rendered absolutely necessary. Then came a new aspirant for a C.B. and Tantia's head, who brought fresh troops and camels into the field. He, perhaps, had not only to chase Tantia, but to keep clear of other forces commanded by a senior in rank to himself. It was wonderful the amount of energy that was thrown into the pursuit, and the hundreds of dead camels strewn over every jungle track: roads were no object, or rivers either, to pursued or pursuers. On they went until dead beaten. Occasionally some one more fortunate than the rest had the luck to catch up the fugitives and cut up stragglers; but it was always in heavy jungle: they had the very best of information, and never trusted themselves to the open country when any force was near. We had the very worst of information, even in the territories of professedly friendly Rajahs. The sympathy of the people was on their side: they appeared to have no difficulty in obtaining supplies, while our columns were sometimes much straitened for grain. The villagers deserted whole tracts of country, and we cut their standing corn for food: not one remained to take the money, and thus it was often said our force was but one degree better than the rebels. This was unavoidable. Occasionally a Bombay column was nearly at Agra, while a Bengal one would touch the Dekkan frontier. Artillery became a useless incumbrance: it necessitated our forces keeping the roads. Ordnance always brought Tantia to grief for the same reason: he found out this fact when General Sir John Mitchel relieved him of the park of artillery which he had stolen from the Rajah of Jalraputtan: he was caught up by the Malwa Division in the stony ravines between Rajghur and Bioura, and lost a score of cannon. He seldom or never used artillery afterwards. So soon as he became very hard pressed, the genuine sepoy left him and slunk off to Hindostan. Tantia was dependant on Velliatees, Bundelas, Bheels, and robbers for his infantry, but they were good shots, and fought well in jungle, attired in green as backwoodsmen. Most of them were mounted on camels and ponies, the latter often shoeless and footsore, their feet bound up with rags to protect them from the rocks. They bivouacked in some deeply-wooded glen at night, and cooked their day's provisions, and slept, but always placed watchful pickets, and seldom could be surprised, and thus were often lost to us for days together. He was beaten often, and as often reported utterly routed. This was a mistake: it was their custom to separate in numerous small bodies when attacked—it facilitated their escape; but they always had their trysting tree, and rallied in a few hours. In one instance they occupied the same encamping ground at night which one of our Regiments had left in the morning. Some of our best Indian Cavalry officers were in pursuit, with Irregular Horse regiments, but could not catch this genius of flight. No one ever saw him even in the distance, until Maun Singh betrayed him to us. Once he made a bold rush past Bhopal across the Nerbudda for the coveted Dekkan, but all was prepared there. There was no wild or planless rushing about. Sir Hugh Rose, who had led triumphant five thousand men from the west of India to the Jumna, through a country teeming with forts, and took them from an enemy fivefold larger in numbers, and disciplined by ourselves and armed with our weapons, was not the man to let the ragged and spirit-broken remnants of Tantia's once-powerful force into the land of the Maharattas. Three lines of defence were formed, and these lines were occupied by bodies of troops, small but close together. The arch-rebel saw it was useless, fled at the sight of the precautionary measures, took the deadly valley of the Tapee for his route, recrossed the Nerbudda, went again towards Rajpootana, and effected a junction with Ferozshah, who brought with him a body of excellent and well-mounted Cavalry. This was but of temporary benefit to them, for every day brought up a fresh force perfectly equipped by the Bombay Government for light and rapid movements, and the rebel chiefs suffered several defeats in quick succession from Generals Mitchel and De Salis, Brigadier Becher, Honnor, and Parke. This induced them to divide into three chief bodies, headed by Tantia, Ferozshah, and the Rao, and then enterprising subalterns took the field with mere handfuls of men, and allowed no peace to the rebels. Scarce a week passed but some band of marauders expiated their crimes, and now all the ashes left, after the burning of this gigantic mutiny, are parties of despicable robbers who fear the light of day.

One advantage reaped by the weary, when a regiment was knocked up and unserviceable, was rest, for considerate Generals would allow ten days in which to recruit our cattle. After two years' nocturnal marching, and daily exposure to the sun or fighting, it is not strange the spirit of weariness should steal over man and horse. Every night's silence, and our sleep, was broken by the same harsh blast of the trumpet, which unwelcome sound forced us to be up and doing. One moment before, all was stillness profound, save the sentry's tread, but now succeeded such confusion or noises, attendant on the falling of tents and loosening of pegs, saddling horses, shouting for servants, trumpeting of elephants, and pitiful moaning of camels; an unearthly light too thrown on all by the heaps of cavalry forage burning—these thousands of ghostly fires, with figures flitting to and fro, lent the character of a spectral world, to be dissipated only by break of day. The supernatural then departed, and we breathed the air of the upper world again—aye, and were troubled with appetites, too, only to be appeased when the long train of baggage had wound its way at a snail's pace into our camp. A week's halt then was trebly welcome, and especially if at the capital of some native prince, as of Jeypoor, where the scenery and architecture excels anything Oriental, or at Kotah, where the officer who loves the field sports of India can enjoy them.

It was the time of winter in India when we entered the latter city and encamped near the half-destroyed bungalows on the right bank of the river Chumbul, and were allowed ten days to refit, and cure the sore backs of our Cavalry horses and baggage animals. The approach and surrounding country is not strikingly beautiful, exhibiting as it does much scrub jungle, of camel-thorn, over a sandy plain full of rain holes and bare sandstone slabs ; but close to the city, which is inside a strong rampart with bastions, and a moat, are magnificent gardens with clusters and avenues of trees of all varieties, from the light and feathery bamboo to the densely foliacious mango. On the east side is a splendid tank, literally covered with wild fowl, and there is marshy ground where the sacred bird of the Egyptians feeds in great numbers. At another part is a large lake, with, one rock in its centre, and on its surface a small summer residence, the very type of beauty and of the picturesque: every detail of its build was reflected with minuteness from the crystal surface of the water beneath it. Here the Rajah could retire from the cares of State, which had been many during the mutiny. Then there was the palace, at the southern extremity of the city, surmounted by domes and cupolas, tapering minarets and towering kiosks, with the unbounded riches of sculpture which make Oriental architecture so attractive. Then there were the splendid pillared and domed monumental buildings raised to commemorate a long line of chieftains, the progenitors of the reigning chief, who is celebrated among his people for his deeds of prowess in arms. These edifices were studded by the family crest, two elephants in deadly combat. Quitting the shade of the giant tamarind trees which grow near, and droop over these abodes of the dead, there was another to be seen, and which lent disquiet to the spirit that would avenge. This was the grave of the Burtons. Father and sons lay side by side with the officers and men who fell during the siege of the city. It is a beautiful graveyard, shady, damp, and green, its walls and tombs overgrown with mosses, lichens, and liver-worts. A mile from this, and the remains of the once beautiful bungalow belonging to Major Burton, stand on the high bank, overlooking the city and river for many miles. Here on its white walls soldiers of pursuing columns, as is their constant custom, have left their autographs, and many other sentiments, in the "no popery" style ; others express the writer's feelings towards mutineers, while some have been moved to poetry. One verse bids the spirits of the Burtons rest, as their blood has been nobly avenged, but its dull Modena-black stain is still on the chunam floor, plain as on the staircase at Holyrood. Now, having heard the particulars of the mournful tragedy at Kotah most feelingly told by a gardener's boy, who apparently had an affection for his late master, we try to forget it, while we give audience to the Rajah's Prime

Minister, who awaits us at our tent with the usual train and offerings of sweetmeats.

The object of the Prime Minister's visit was, to enquire after the health of the Commandant of our Force, and ask at what hour the Rajah should visit our camp. As the sun was going down, he appeared escorted by the greater part of his army, equipped in the most motley style, and marching in a most disorderly manner to a very noisy march played by his band, in which the number of European and native instruments about equalled each other, and some English march and "Taza be taza" seemed to be struggling for the mastery. However, the individual who carried the English drum belaboured it so fearfully, that I gave the casting vote in favor of the opinion that English tunes were in the ascendant. Had Jullien been present when the native air predominated, he would have failed to discover its similarity to "the well-known Brahmin Hymn:" there was no measured tread keeping time, but a general shuffling, scuffling noise of men and horses. First came the Cavalry, fat ghee-fed men on fatter horses, with their heads bound down by standing martingales, and performing all kinds of antics impossible to an

English horse, besides rearing, jumping like deers, or walking on their hind legs: order was immaterial. Occasionally a horseman would dash from rear to front whirling his spear, and appearing a very Ajax. The men were dressed in every possible colour, and armed variously. Then came the Infantry, such a set of ill-looking men, armed with sword and matchlock, with matches burning. Many of them were dressed as British soldiers, in red coats and pipe-clayed belts, and carried some old flint muskets which must have done duty in the days of Lord Clive; but the Commander-in-Chief, who had evidently had choice of the piece of cloth from which these red coats had been made for his own particular wear, had selected the selvage on which the quality of the cloth had been printed in letters of gilt, so that the greater part of the word "superfine" appeared on the back of his red coat in large letters four or five inches square; he was not a very tall man, and there was not quite enough room for the last three letters of the word. I looked for these on the coat of his aide-de-Camp, but could not see them. Next came the Rajah's chantry priests immediately in front of him, singing his praises in a monotonous tune and invoking blessings on his head : from their looks cast towards us, I could not help fancying they were cursing us occasionally. Now came the Rajah, preceded by his led charger gorgeously caparisoned. Such a moving mass of fat, he resembled the monsters of Smithfield : the carbon of sugar-cane and ghee came oosing through his skin at every motion. Then came the great man himself, carried on men's shoulders in a species of sedan chair, and condescendingly acknowledging the salaams and genuflexions of his subjects, who crowded round him, for there are parasites in native states. Now the Rajah's figure was portly, but his countenance unprepossessing. He seemed to have lost one eye, perhaps in war, the plough of the nobler passions had left no furrows on his brow, he seldom smiled, but appeared friendly. Next in order came more infantry, and, finally, two small cannon horsed: they were without limbers. The gunners were all mounted, one carrying a sponge-staff jauntily over his shoulders, another a smoking match. The ceremony passed with the usual meaningless compliments and flowery nothings, and it became our turn to visit him.

Accordingly about 4 P. M., after furbishing up our ragged uniforms, the officers of our force, with an escort of Cavalry, proceeded to his palace on the opposite side of the town, which we observed bore but few marks of having been besieged: here and there was the impression of a round-shot on some building. The merlons, which had been knocked to pieces, were all rebuilt, and the guns on the ramparts in good order. We proceeded through about a mile of narrow streets, when we arrived at the portal of the palace enclosure, and, dismounting, we were conducted into a quadrangular tilt-yard within the building. Here on one side was a raised platform of great size canopied with scarlet: at one end of this, in full Durbar dress, sat the Rajah with his interpreter. In his lap lay a most elaborate sword and shield: the admiration we shewed towards these pleased him, and he ordered a nautch. Now nautches are well enough in the day-time, if the girls are attractive, but these were not even passable: same want of *beauty* was observable in Scindiah's nautch girls on the occasion of his return to his throne. This would have been far less apparent by torchlight, and we were rather glad when the

Kotah girls were permitted to cease their music and dancing. To this succeeded the process of decorating each of us with a garland of white mogree flowers, which was placed round our necks. The greatest among us had to wear two. It was amusing to watch the expressions of officers' faces as they were being thus bedizened like so many children who had been out daisying in the meadows of England. This ludicrous scene was terminated by our being sprinkled with rose water and anointed with attar, the smell of which pertinaciously clung to our jackets for weeks afterwards.

Next we proceeded, the Rajah leading, through a series of narrow passages blackened by the smoke of torches, and bringing the pit entrance to Drury Lane forcibly to one's memory ; and then, by ascending some steep flights of steps, we gained the cool rooms on the top of the palace. These were beautifully and tastefully furnished, the walls of elaborately sculptured white marble, and one room was appropriated to Oriental paintings. The view from these upper stories was beautifully picturesque and extensive. It was his favorite resort, where to enjoy music, marble, melancholy, and moonlight.

We could not admire his pictures, and descended to some balconies overlooking the elephant pens, as he had promised to show us an elephant fight.

Below us was a fine male, with huge tusks mounted with iron rings to preserve them from splitting, and his hind legs bound with massive chains to the wall, and tethered together with cables, so that he was unable to move aught save his head, trunk, and fore legs: separating him from the court-yard without was a stout, broad wall of masonry. He was in a state of great excitement, and kept his attention fixed on a gate by which his antagonist was to enter. This sport was evidently a favorite pastime of that Rajah's, and after some moments of expectation on our part, as well as of that of the huge beast below us, his antagonist appeared in the gateway, and, as soon as he sighted his pent-up fellow, rushed on ere the charge, trunk uplifted and trumpetting furiously. The other, his small eyes lit up by the fire of rage, and with a tail terrific to dwell upon, dashed forward so far as his tethers admitted, and a collision between the leviathan skulls took place, giving out a loud, dull, sickening sound, while their tusks crushed and splintered against each other with a noise as of an oak tree riven by lightning. The attacking elephant was now goaded by a band of spearmen, who separated them, to allow a fresh charge to be made, and the same scene was repeated: once the charging animal missed his aim, and the other with his trunk held his antagonist's head down on the wall, and tried to drag him over it. Had these two noble beasts been free to fight without the interposed barrier, the scene would have been a desperate one. It was a barbarous sport, worthy of a barbarous people: we were not pleased by it, and as it had now become dusk, we bade adieu to the Rajah, and marched by the light of flaring torches to our camp.

On the morrow, hearing the Chumbul abounded in fish, we took our tackle, two of us, and dropped down the river alongside the town in a large ferry boat, and prepared to enjoy a little of the innocent and moral amusement of catching fish. Almost the whole length of the town, flights of shallow steps ran down to the water's edge—the river here is deep and blue; thousands of women washing and bathing were studded over them: the many-coloured skirts and shawls as worn by the fair Rajpoot women rendered the scene equal to that on the Grand Canal of Venice. The sport must have exceeded that obtainable any where, for no sooner had the bait been cast on the waters, than it was seized by a monster fish far too heavy for our tackle; nevertheless we had but helped one over the boat's edge than another dashed away with our lines. We soon succeeded in covering the bottom of our ferry boat with fish weighing from one to sixteen or eighteen pounds each : at last we were compelled to cease, our rods having been broken into splinters, and our hooks entirely expended. Just as we were returning, the Rajah sent us a message to say they were fish petted, fed, and held sacred by the Brahmins which we had been catching, and asked us to go further from the town. Of course we were in ignorance of the fact, but it enabled us to account for the angry looks of the Gossains, who had seen the excellent sport. We did not therefore go again, but turned our attention to hunting wild pig, and by daybreak next morning it was our lot to go into preserved ground again.

Wending our way towards the site of the old

Kotah Residency, we took the open country, and came to a patch of jungle about a mile square, surrounded by a low wall. We had scarcely entered it when we saw a herd of about twenty wild hogs. We could not get them to break cover; and searched for others, which were soon found: we selected the largest, rode him, and my companion speared him. As we stood admiring him, within a short distance of us there passed one of the largest boars I ever saw. I set out alone after him, and speared him three times, and on the last occasion left one half of my weapon sticking through his grisly body: he made a furious onslaught, upsetting my horse and self, and having narrowly escaped with my life, I had the mortification to see him trot away with about a yard of my spear protruding from his back. He was bleeding fast, but I had no other weapon, and gave up the combat to return to our trophy, which between us, assisted by a native, we carried to the nearest village, no easy task. Of course, we expected friendship so near Kotah, and aid to carry home the spoil, but the inhabitants assailed us in such numbers with stones and threats, that we were obliged to retreat. On telling the Rajah of our sport, we found we had been to his preserve! He promised to recover the animal's cranium and broken spear for us. About midday we received a hurried message from him, saying a tiger had just slain a bullock on the river bank and waited to be killed. We seized our rifles and took boat down the river, opposite the palace. The Rajah himself joined us in his pleasure boat, with a numerous and gaily-dressed suite, armed with most elaborately gilt matchlocks : he himself was provided with an English rifle. In a second boat was the band before alluded to. Aided by the stream we soon accomplished eight miles on the river, which runs through a deep channel of old red sandstone, forming itself into bold rocky scenery, some times masses protruded above the surface of the stream, and on these alligators and huge river tortoises basked in the sun. We were rather amused at being told, that on a former occasion, when Kotah was visited by a force, the officers of the staff killed and eat them. We hoped it was a mistake. On our way we saw one small tiger, scarce larger than a pointer dog, but did not molest it. On arriving at the ravine running down to the water, where the tiger was reported to be, we drew our boats up opposite and then some two hundred *shikarrees*, previously concealed, formed line and swept down the ravine, firing off matchlocks, every report of which was repeated by the echoes of a hundred rocky caverns. We awaited the appearance of the tiger in great impatience, but saw him not: they told us he had broken back through the line, and I subsequently heard almost all officers visiting Kotah had been invited to kill that accommodating tiger, therefore inferred he was a sort of unicorn or mythical beast. But the trip and scenery amply rewarded us. The band struck up: its harshness was softened by the water and distance. We went over to the Rajah's boat, and amused ourselves by shooting at the alligators, and talking with him on the merits of fire-arms: arrived at the palace stairs, we wished him good-bye, and received another wreath of rose and jasmine. On the next day we left Kotah, and joined again in pursuit of Tantia.

CHAPTER XI.

TANTIA'S DESCENT ON JALRAPUTTAN—ACTION AT RAJGHUR—AND CAPTURE OF THE REBEL ARTILLERY PARK—WEATHERBOUND—ACTION AT MUNGROWLEE—ACTION AT SINDWAHO—AFFAIR AT KURAI.

TANTIA TOPEE, after his severe handling at Gwalior by Sir Hugh Rose, and in its neighbourhood by some of his successors, resorted to "fresh fields and pastures new," and came down into Central India, first honouring Jalraputtan with a visit. The Rajah of that place fled to his seraglio, and afterwards to an English force at Soosneer, for safety; his soldiery, previously in heart, and now in person, joined the mutineers, and increased their numbers to 10,000 men, who were tolerably imposing in appearance, being well off for clothes and treasure, while they took nearly two score of cannon from the Rajah's city and fort, and then marched leisurely to Rajghur.

Colonel Lockhart, who was in command of a force at Soosneer, moved eastward, and at Nulkeera was joined by General Michel and some troops from Mhow, and it was suspected Tantia cast longing eyes on the city of Bhopal; but Captain Hutchinson, Political Agent of that territory, procured intelligence of the movement of the rebels on Rajghur, and General Michel, after marching from 4 A. M. to 4 P. M., came in sight of them on an eminence near the town. They were then in the act of pitching their camp: but the Infantry part of the Force, consisting of the 22nd and part of the 72nd Highlanders, 4th Rifles, and 19th B. N. I., were so knocked up by the day's march that they were unable to go further, though the 19th Regt. volunteered to come on alone. They were all three miles in rear of the mounted soldiery, who were now retired to recruit until the morrow; and a picket of Cavalry was placed to watch. The rebels threw out one likewise; we threw out videttes, so did the rebels, but two to our one. As the main body of our troops was about to encamp, an old woman was observed prowling about, and taking more observations than old women generally do, when a trooper of the 3rd Bombay

Light Cavalry suspected the apparent sex of the creature was not the real one, and the old lady's head-dress being removed, disclosed an extensive pair of whiskers, so that the individual was made to pay for his temerity by forfeiting his life.

Both forces held the above described position till dawn, Tantia having anticipated a defeat by sending his loot off to Mucksoodnugger in the evening. At 3 A. M., in silence, we left our encampment, and advanced, but the enemy had gone. On our nearing the town the Rajah came out on a prancing horse to make his obeisance to the Major-General, and on being asked to point out a road by which we might pass the town and river, showed us one by which single horsemen could only descend with great difficulty, but the aide-de-camp quickly discovered a wide road and ford, which the Rajah seemed to wish to conceal. The Cavalry, composed of three weak squadrons of H. M.'s 17th Lancers, and two of the Bombay 3rd Light Cavalry under Sir W. Gordon, pushed forward to reconnoitre, and made a general movement to the front; while considerable excitement began to pervade the force, heightened by the sight of a few of the enemy's horsemen in the jungle on the Bioura road. General Michel advanced with the Cavalry to ascertain Tantia's position, while the Artillery and Infantry breakfasted. The position of his cavalry was discerned to be in line on a hill amidst much brushwood and jungle, and they in turn sent out two of their officers and about sixty troopers, who advanced down the face of the hill towards us, but as our small numbers did not admit of investigation, the General ordered a troop of the 3rd Light Cavalry forward in skirmishing order to drive them back. This was done by a cornet of that corps, whose ardour led him on some distance until he came in sight of one of the enemy's guns. Collecting seven or eight of the troopers nearest him, he made a dash at it and took it, again pressing on, accompanied by an officer of the 17th Lancers and a few of the 3rd Bombay troopers who had been able to keep pace; when suddenly this zealous but small band emerged on an open plateau where the enemy had placed two pieces of cannon, two hundred infantry, and about sixty sowars. They opened a volley of musketry, and about forty of the cavalry pursued, for our small party had been obliged to ride for their lives, and indeed the cornet was not far in advance of a very long spear carried by one of the rebel horsemen, who seemed bent on making use of it, but luckily the sight of the Lancers, who had been steadily coming up, caused him and his fellows to rejoin their force, which had been unknowingly passed to our right, so thick was the brushwood hereabouts ; moreover the ground was undulating and stony. The Lancers now went left wheel, and our Artillery came up, and a harmless cannonade commenced; but our adversary had the best of the range, possessing 3 guns and a 13-inch mortar, whereas we had but four light field pieces. They managed to shoot away the top of a dooly in which was carried the breakfast of some of the officers of the 19th Regiment ; the bearers were unhurt, but greatly astonished. The Infantry on moving from the river where they had breakfasted, discovered a party of rebels who had been missed by the Cavalry. These sought the water and dived like amphibia ; but, unlike that division of the animal kingdom, possessed no apparatus for respiring in the new element, and were obliged to come to the surface and be shot. When the rebel army saw our entire Force advancing, they commenced a retreat on Bioura, and were sorely pressed by our Cavalry, but our Infantry fell out in great numbers, fatigued by the heat of the day, it being now one o'clock. Seven guns were abandoned in one nullah. The pursuit was continued until 5 P. M. within four miles of Bioura, the whole of Tantia's park of twenty-seven guns having been captured, and many of the enemy killed. The Lancers and 3rd Bombay Cavalry halted under the shade of some trees, and Lieutenant Shaw, who had received a sun-stroke, died there.

General Michel's Force now halted a day, and the 4th Rifles took the captured guns to Indore, and Captain Mayne, with a regiment of irregular horse from Goonah, joined the force. Tantia, exasperated at the loss of his guns, marched through the densely jungle-covered district of Mocksoodnuggur to Seronge, and blew away his own adjutant general of artillery from the muzzle of a cannon. The Mhow troops now followed in pursuit, passing through Nursinghur; but between this place and Birseeah the monsoon set in with such force that they were obliged to halt—and this was no uncommon occurrence with the forces in the field at this season, which were engaged in the chase over a heavy country. Such an amount of rain would fall that pursued and pursuers could move no further. On one occasion when this happened, the rebel force was barely five miles distant, and knew perfectly well they were safe. Sometimes a Quarter Master General would pitch the camp in low ground, which from the downpour of rain would become perfectly flooded, and every step one took was knee deep in black mud. Nothing could be more miserable work for man or beast than this being weatherbound. First the heavens would assume a dungeon-like darkness, and the air become close and sultry, and then be followed by torrents of rain borne on such hurricanes of wind that the tents and ropes shrank and drew their pegs and bushes, and from their weight came squash down on the unfortunate occupants, whose forms could be seen heaving and struggling under the weight of the wet canvas, vainly endeavouring to get from beneath it, and the state of the weather such that no one would go to their assistance. A soldier who has not experienced this calamity knows nothing of the amount of misery it entails on the victim. Every article he possesses, including bed and bedding, is drenched, and the canvas dwelling so heavy with rain and mud that it refuses to be erected again; and you can now sympathise with your wretched horses as they stand crouching rear to the wind, and tails between their legs, not able to lie down in the water, now running in rivulets beneath them; and, to complete the chapter of wretchedness, you see your cooking rowtee has followed the example of your tent, and in its fall extinguished the cook, fires, dinner, and all, and the hot meal you had looked on as the only bright speck in your day's existence, vanishes into a gloomy perspective. Some more fortunate friend hails you, and clutching your papers and sword you retreat into his better drained tent, sharing his dry clothes until midnight, when through the unabated rain and thick darkness you have to go your "rounds," visiting the various pickets round about and guards in the interior of the camp. A few hours' sunshine soon enables one to move again.

When the rain had a trifle abated its fury on the tents of the Mhow force, Captain Mayne with his regiment followed Tantia to Esaughur, and halted twelve miles distant, and on the approach of Brigadier Smith, commanding the Sipree Brigade, marched twenty-five miles to the north-west, and the Brigadier moved eight miles to meet him. In the mean time the rebels had beaten Scindiah's troops under the Shah Subah of Easaughur, and took from thence two guns which they abandoned on a hill near the town, and completely sacked it. Brigadier Smith on arriving at Esaughur saw the rear guard of the rebels leaving it; the main body had gone to Mungrowlee, but a few of the better mounted had marched towards Ranode, the direction Captain Mayne would have taken, had he not joined Brigadier Smith.

General Michel had brought his Force from Seronge, and was just pitching his camp at Mungrowlee, when a picket galloped in, reporting the rebels to be close at hand. The General had but eighty-eight effective lancers. With these, his guns, and infantry, he moved out, and on a small hill to the northward was the advanced guard of Tantia, and in their rear his entire force, quite unaware of our proximity. Le-Marchand opened his guns on them, the shot dropping into the advanced guard: and our force formed up in order of battle, while Tantia huddled his masses into the best shape the limited time and surprise gave him. Suddenly an alarm-cry was raised in our rear, while Tantia's masses began to give way. Sir William Gordon and fifty of his men galloped to ascertain the cause of alarm, which proved to be not entirely without foundation. A party of Velliattees were displaying great bravery against six unarmed dooly bearers, who were carrying a man of the Highlanders wounded in the leg: he was killed by them, and the bearers wounded. The arrival of the lancers caused them suddenly to disappear in the heavy jungle, and Sir W. Gordon after some difficulty espied their heads among the foliage. Any order in advancing through such disadvantageous ground was impossible, but the words "Open out and pursue at a gallop" were no sooner given, than the fifty brave fellows of his squadron, regardless of bush or briar, were among the treacherous Velliattees, and accounted for upwards of eighty of their number; neither did the lancers return till their spears were covered with gore, their leader having killed three of the four-score. As the force advanced against the rebel front, one of their wounded, and a man of some importance among them, while being moved away on a charpoy was abandoned, and had to watch our line advancing on him; he had been a subedar in the Bengal Infantry. The officers of the 19th Regiment N. I. discovered he was labouring from the effects of a bullet wound in the thigh: he opened the breast of his coat, took out a handkerchief, blindfolded himself, and requested to be shot. The rebels fled across the Betwa to the Tal Behut jungles, leaving three hundred dead on the field, while the General had taken six guns and many prisoners from them; and considering his inferior numbers, it was a brilliant affair.

The rebels having now entered Bundlekund, it was determined to follow them with three columns of troops, the right or Infantry column under Colonel Lockhart, the centre composed of Cavalry under Colonel De Salis, and the left Infantry column with two guns and some native Cavalry attached was commanded by Brigadier Smith. The centre column on gaining the river Betwa halted to construct a ghaut, the rebels having crossed it tumultuously, and probably floundered through it in a way unbecoming the dignity of British troops. It was the intention of the General, who with the divisional staff accompanied this column, to advance due east after passing the river, but Captain Mayne, who had gone on ahead with his Regiment in order to ascertain the state of the roads and their freedom or otherwise from rebels, was fired on by Bundeelas in a difficult and jungly pass leading to Jaolone. Intelligence of this route being infested by these troublesome denizens of the jungle, induced the Major-General to make forced marches south and join the column under Colonel Lockhart, which he did at Narut, and from thence the force would have moved in a direction North-west towards Lullutpore, but at one o'clock on the following morning intelligence was received of the rebels moving across our front in order to loot Tehree, and that on the previous evening they had reached and halted at Sindwaho, about fifteen miles north of Narut. Our course was again changed in consequence, and at daybreak arrived in sight of one of the enemy's pickets under a cluster of trees near Sindwaho. On seeing our advance the enemy's sowars sprang on their horses and galloped to their camp to give intelligence. We continued to advance, and near the village the whole of Tantia's force was visible, and in excellently chosen position; and while our four guns with a strong escort maintained a centre position, Colonel de Salis advanced with the Cavalry to the right, in order to feel the enemy's left and cut off their retreat from Tehree. At this moment the enemy opened a rapid and well-directed artillery fire, causing many casualties among a squadron of the 3rd Bombay Cavalry. Several shots were directed on them especially; one fell under the left troop leader's horse and the following shot killed three horses immediately behind him. Tantia's Infantry advanced towards our guns, while his cavalry hovered round ours, which consisted of troops of the 8th Hussars, 17th Lancers, Bombay Lancers, and 3rd Light Cavalry with a squadron of Mayne's Horse. Sir William Gordon with men of his corps, and of the 8th Hussars and Bombay Lancers, so soon as the Infantry had fired a volley, charged; six guns were captured, and the killed numbered upwards of five hundred men. They also captured the palanquin belonging to the Nawab of Banda. There were fresh blood stains in its interior, but we learnt subsequently the blood was not that of the Nawab, as he gave himself up shortly afterward to General Michel, and his skin was entire. Several women, too, were taken, and one so attractive that either her beauty or blandishments won the heart of a native soldier of the force who requested premission to wed her. Soon after the decisive charge had taken place, the 3rd Bombay Light Cavalry were in support of two guns on the left and near a field of high jowarree, when they observed a body of the rebels emerge from it, who opened a galling musketry fire on the troopers and wounded several horses. The officer commanding retired them from their too close proximity, and the rebels formed into a rude square or *gole*, being composed of Bengal sepoys of the 36th Regiment and Velliattees. An officer of the Lancers doing duty with the 3rd Bombay Cavalry, on seeing them, attacked them singly and alone, commencing with a Velliattee, who chanced to be the corner man, while the others stood at the charge with musket and bayonet unwilling to move from their formation, in which they seemed to feel security. The Velliattee having escaped the first blow aimed at him, drew a two-handed sword and made a furious onslaught, but as he in turn missed his aim he fell beneath the officer's charger, and was now in a fair way to be pinned to the earth, but rose again to the fight. At this crisis (and it was rather a serious one with the gallant young soldier who attacked them) a young trooper of the 3rd Bombay Cavalry charged to the rescue; the Velliattee immediately turned his attention on him, and aimed a blow which grazed his back, severed the horse's crupper and part of the saddle, sinking deep into the spine of the animal. The trooper's well-aimed blow clove the skull of the rebel. Three of the group now threw down their arms and shouted for forgiveness, but the next was for fighting, and the officer now engaged him. He clubbed his musket with the bayonet fixed, and as he raised it to deliver a ponderous blow the point caught in the drapery of his waist, delayed the descent of the musket butt, and at the same time exposed his chest to a thrust which ran completely through him. By this time the troopers of the 3rd Light Cavalry had arrived and finished the work so well begun.

On no occasion in the pursuit did Tantia's men fight so well as at Sindwaho. Our Cavalry had been on the saddle from 2 A. M. until 5 P. M., and were glad to encamp and halt a day. The rebels were prevented going to Tehree. After this engagement the force marched on Lullutpoor, and encamped some distance from the village, and a *russud* guard of Tantia's entered it unaware of our proximity. The Cavalry mounted, and scouring the country captured some carts and animals laden with ammunition. Tantia at this time was hard pressed and was driven to a desperate move. He marched his force from north of Lullutpoor to Kurai, passing within four miles of us, and between our position and the river Betwa, while we, not knowing it, also passed near his camp. Our Infantry had to make long marches to keep pace with the enemy, and many of our soldiers were almost shoeless. From Lullutpoor we marched to Multowa, and from thence to a village near Khimlassa where the enemy had been just previously. Leaving this we proceeded twelve miles to Kurai, and while debouching from the town on to the plain, saw Tantia's army in full march southward. The part visible to us we concluded to be their front, but subsequently found the major part had gone on, and those in sight were infantry, and men mounted on tattoos, numbering about two thousand, too tired to keep pace with Tantia. Our left shoulder was now brought up, and as we advanced they appeared induced to stand, but not liking the steady and solid apperance of our line they broke and fled, and a pursuit was commenced. Three bodies of Cavalry started, led by Captains Sir W. Gordon, Mayne, and Colonel Curtis—the two former came on the greatest number of fugitives. Mayne's Horse and the 3rd Cavalry under Captain Oldfield killed about one hundred and fifty in a pursuit over six miles, during which a sepoy who had turned to fight saw an officer approach to kill him and shouted, "Do not kill me, it is not a Sahib's duty. I intend to fight and may kill you." The Sahib, however, lodged two pistol bullets in him, when he was surrounded by troopers and fought with great bravery until despatched. This affair of Kurai did much to discomfit and separate the rebels, as well causing an estimated loss of three hundred and fifty to them. So much were they separated by these engagements, that after Sindwaho those that were driven north never joined Tantia again; some took service with Maun Singh, others followed the wake of Tantia and crossed the Nerbudda, taking refuge and dispersing in the Putchmurree hills, others hung about the valleys of the Taptee and Nerbudda rivers, affording amusement to the Jaulnah Field Force under Colonel Beatson, while the main body, Tantia, and the treasure marched to Bagrode.

CHAPTER XII.

COLONEL BECHER'S ENGAGEMENT WITH TANTIA'S CAVALRY AT BAGRODE—A NIGHT ALARM—TANTIA CROSSES THE NERBUDDA—A HALT AT BHOPAL—TANTIA ON THE MARCH—HE ATTEMPTS SIR HUGH ROSE'S LINE OF DEFENCE ON THE DEKKAN FRONTIER.

ON the 25th of October we marched on Kurgowlee, which was but eight miles distant. The whole country was deserted, and we could not get a single person to show us the road, for, be it known, in this part of the country roads are mere tracks, such as sheep make, and, steering by the sun, we reached our destination, but had gone a circuit of fourteen miles across country. A despatch found its way to us in the course of the day, ordering us to Bagrode, and from thence to Ratghur, an old familiar spot to those who served under Sir Hugh Rose. Direction, or distance, were alike immaterial to us, for we lived a nomadic life, and were always on the move, so that we shot peafowl, colon, and antelope by the way, and marched always in the daytime. Being without Europeans we could afford to disregard the sun. That night we had just made our evening meal, and laid down to sleep, having, as was our custom, sent forward a *russud* guard to provide forage against our arrival at Bagrode on the morrow, when we heard a hubbub in camp and the trumpet calling to horse, and not wishing to be attacked while undressed, we hurried on our accoutrements and mounted, and then learnt that as our *russud* guard had entered the town of Bagrode, they had found it occupied by Tantia's followers, who were coolly walking off with the forage and stores laid there for us. Our men of course made a speedy exit, and hid in some jungle, on a hill from which Tantia's camp could be seen. They made an estimate (probably exaggerated) that there were 10,000 men, and numbers of elephants, camels, and other beasts of burden. Two of our horsemen returned to tell us, and we were now going to the rescue. We were obliged to abandon our baggage, pretty much to the charge of a vast troop of monkeys, which swarmed in the trees there, for we numbered but three hundred raw mercenary troops, and scarce one knew the use of his weapons, and, of course, there was a possibility they might not trouble to use them. Nevertheless we marched within three miles of the rebel camp, when the road became covered by jungle, and, scarcely daring to trust ourselves in such disadvantageous ground, we struck across the Saugor road in more open country, and occupied a gorge in the hills, through which we heard the enemy would pass in early morning, and we agreed to stay and wait here, and "see what turned up," fondly hoping that it would be a couple of field guns, which was the very modest reinforcement we had applied for to attack 10,000 men. The night was bitterly cold, with a nasty biting wind blowing, and, tired of inaction, we determined to send two spies into the camp to ascertain the feasibility of a night attack on the rebels. Two sowars immediately volunteered, disguised themselves as peasants, and left for the camp. We anxiously awaited their return, but they never came. Next day we saw two headless trunks, which accounted for it. In fact, it became evident Tantia knew of our proximity. Guns were fired from all Scindiah's police stations down the road as warning signals to the enemy. Day broke, and we could see a distance of twenty miles in the direction our cannon should come, and none appearing, we withdrew from the gorge into the plain behind it, and while so doing, heard Tantia and the Rao Sahib had gone off immediately on hearing of our arrival. We then marched into Bagrode, picketted our horses, and ascended a hill hard by, affording a good view of the country, having been assured by the vakeel not a trace of a rebel was near the place; but, no sooner had we raised our field glasses, than a large body of cavalry appeared drawn up in line about a mile and a half distant, and from their vary-coloured dresses we knew them as rebel troops. We hastened down the hill and mounted, and in an instant our gallant Commandant was leading at a dashing pace towards them. Our troopers behaved right well, being, if anything, too eager. The rebel rank remained perfectly steady until we were close on them, when they broke and fled. We were amongst them, and pursued them across bad nullahs, broken ground, and high grass for a distance of five miles, the Adjutant and Assistant Surgeon leading. Above forty were cut down or speared, when it was necessary to draw rein, as it was possible to be cut off by some other parties of the enemy. The hog spears we carried, manufactured by Bodraj, Aurungabad, and mounted on bamboos, proved invaluable weapons, though they actually curved when they struck the hard skulls of the rebel horsemen, who were mostly well mounted, and had gold mohurs and ornaments concealed about them. The precious metal proved a great attraction to loot the bodies, in which achievement irregular horse excel. We had but one man severely sabred, but lost several horses. We subsequently learnt this party of rebels had marched forty miles that day, expecting to find Tantia at Bagrode, and mistook our camp for his until we went out to attack them. Returning to our camp, we found a hussar, who belonged to one of the numerous pursuing columns, but had lost his way and luckily fell in with friends. We remained very watchful through the night, thinking it possible Tantia might come down to take his revenge, as we knew he could not be far distant. Next day we marched on Gwarispore, and arrived just in time to save the travellers' bungalow being burnt. The kansamah had already departed, taking with him the plates, dishes, and cooking utensils, and was hiding in a ravine near. On finding out we were not the rebel force, which we closely assimilated in appearance, the men being entirely without uniform, and their clothes ragged from wear, he came out and welcomed us. We were none the less glad to see him, not having eaten since the night previously. We did not pay the customary tribute of one rupee each person for bungalow hire, considering we had done well to save it from destruction; but a heartless Post-master, some months afterwards, sent us the bill, insinuating the hussar, who had not left his name, should pay his toll also. We now marched on Bhopal with all haste, as our spies brought us intelligence Tantia was determined to advance on that city, and though we did not number so many hundreds as the rebel host had thousands, we determined to frustrate his plans. We travelled parallel to each other, a range of hills separating us, and slept at Bhilsa. About midnight men from our pickets galloped in, stating that an immense force had arrived, and threatened to put us all to the sword. We doubted the report altogether, but the small arm firing getting so fast and furious, we began to think the rebels had in truth arrived. It was intensely dark. We mounted and rode off to the spot where the fight seemed to have begun. Our presence restored confidence, and silence, for the fight was all with ourselves —not a vestige of an opponent could we see or hear in the deep gloom. The simple fact was, that the recollected images of Tantia's troops were, by the excited state of our troopers' minds, rendered more vivid than actual impressions, and hence the alarm. So we retired and slept unmolested until morning, when we were up and on our way to Bhopal. Here we fell in with another flying column, which had also come with a view to save the city, the rebel army having, by a feint, drawn over the Nerbudda river another regiment of irregular horse which was waiting for them, and then crossed over themselves, giving its brave young commandant the trouble of recrossing; and, by the time gained, Tantia was in a fair way of being first at the treasury of Baitool, having relinquished his plan of occupying Bhopal.

We were glad to see the gilded minarets of

Her Highness the Begum's palace, as they glittered in the sunshine amidst the groves of trees which ornament her capital, for she always gave the most cordial welcome and energetic support to British officers and troops. No sooner are our tents pitched in one of her gardens of orange, citron, and rose bushes, and studded with buildings, pillared and domed, each chronicling some mythological event, than a train of servants appears, bringing us a meal that would have done honor to the halls of Lucullus. There were stews, curries, pilaus, sweetmeats, and fruits, of endless variety, with the usual enquiries for the state of our health, and a polite invitation to the palace at 3 P. M. At that time the state elephants, with their gorgeous trappings and howdahs, came to convey us there, and we started with a large escort of her troops swelled by our own native officers, all gorgeously dressed in the tinsel and daub of colour a native loves so well. We passed through the city, abounding in buildings and objects one craved to stay and sketch, and, arriving at the palace courtyard, we passed the household troops. One could not divest one's mind of their being dummies dressed in European uniform ready for the battle at Astley's, or to heighten the effect of one of Kean's tragedies. Their dresses hung awkwardly about their ill-chosen bodies, as they presented arms with a ludicrous pomposity. But now we dismount, down go the mammoth's hind-quarters, and we convulsively clutch the howdah rail to prevent being shot out behind, to the serious detriment of one's plumed helmet. Descending at length, we are conducted through a series of dark passages and low stair-cases, which render the light of several torches necessary, though it is broad daylight without. The smell of these, and the sooty state of the walls coated by the smoke from them, render it rather a strange approach to those unused to visit native royalty. Having emerged from the smoke-laden air on the top of the palace, we find ourselves on a large flat roof, covered with red cloth, and surrounded by soft cushions. Here we are received by the chief engineer or superintendant of Her Highness' public works, and conducted to her presence. She received us with much cordiality, unveiled, as is her custom, and attended by one only of her sex: we are four white, or rather sunburnt, faces inclined to red, attended by about thirty or forty dark ones.

All are accommodated with seats, the usual compliments are passed, and a most loyal harangue is delivered to our dusky friends, a speech which showed Her Highness to be far before her fellow creatures in intelligence and sound common sense. Our attention was now invited to the magnificent prospect from her window over the lake of Bhopal, which extends three or four miles, beautifully shaded by a wooded hill on one side, and on the other covered by the mangrove, bulrush, and water lily, and teeming with wild fowl. At rest beneath the palace was a steam boat, scarcely so large as one of the penny denizens of the Thames: this was reserved for an after inspection, and we now had an opportunity to survey the state apartment. It was a long, narrow, and low room, covered with Persian carpets, and had a ceiling cloth of gay damask, while the greater part of its space was taken up by a long English dining-room style of table, covered with vases, artificial flowers, toys, dissolving views in a globular vessel of alabaster, such as are shown you for the small sum of a ha'p'ny by the pensioners on the hill at Greenwich, together with a variety of articles of English manufacture, like indeed those that would be collected for a few shillings in the Lowther Arcade. Lastly, but not least attractive, was a musical box, which was wound up and ran down, its spicular roller having reminded us of "Auld Lang Syne," "Robin Adair," and the four other tunes so usual in those boxes—the last, of course, our National Anthem, always welcome, and worthy all occasions. Now a small box of French manufacture, ingenious and frivolous as those who made it, was brought to our notice: the spring being touched, a small but perfect bird of the singing genus hopped on its lid, and delivered itself most melodiously. This engrossed the native portion of the audience, who sat wrapt in admiration. It was indeed a clever piece of mechanism. While listening to the bird's song, I had involuntarily put in my mouth a piece of betel and pan, with which we had been supplied in great plenty: the lime burned, the cardamom stung, and the bitters ness of the green leaf contributed to my misery. In vain did I protrude my tongue beneath my moustache, that the breeze wafted from the lake through the royal apartment might cool it, and I was extremely thankful when Her Highness proposed we should take coffee, which was served in *English china*, and the liquid of most delicious flavour. This made myself and my palate friends again, and I readily acquiesced to a trip in the steamer. Conducted by the Engineer (who spoke English) to its anchorage, we embarked, and steamed to the further extremity of the lake, being well paid for our excursion by the magnificent scenery, which is one of the characteristics of the surrounding geological formation—the old red Sandstone, as we left the shore, dotted by its picturesque, and very varied architecture, and alive with its gaily dressed people, every creature, and building, reflected in the glassy surface of the lake. I thought I had never seen aught so beautiful. We had time to learn the history of the vessel, and how Captain Keatinge, Political Agent of Nemar, had imported it from England, fitted it, and taught the stokers how to drive it. We learnt indeed all the Begum's engineer, a most intelligent native, could detail, and listened to the old familiar cries of the call boys, "Ease her!" "Back her!" and "Stop her!" We returned, and landed at dusk, the inhabitants flocking to the shore to have a stare at us; when our Commandant asked the engineer if the steamer had not caused much amazement among them, and whether he ever vouchsafed an explanation of its propelling power, but he evidently was of opinion,

"A little learning is a dangerous thing,"

and showed a supreme contempt for the unenlightened state of his fellow citizens by replying, "Why should I teach the brute creation ?" He was indeed determined the Pierian spring should not be tasted by them. Her Highness the Begum insisted we should not leave until we had seen her palace lit up: we therefore returned, and bade her adieu amidst a galaxy of small lights, and left her, unable to explain why three of us, who had passed the age of twenty, should still be bachelors.

We returned to camp, and were off again in the night after Tantia, but this time with the addition of European Dragoons, and a commissariat on hackeries. These were fatal to our progress at speed, while the civil authorities were clamorous in urging us on to save Baitool. We crossed the Nerbudda in all haste at Hooshungabad, the Irregular Cavalry made forced marches on ahead, and arrived at the threatened treasury just in time, the rebel army being but fourteen miles distant, at Mooltye, which district they had entered with much pomp and noise, announcing, by proclamation, they were but the advanced guard of the Peishwa's force, which was returning from its numberless victories in Central India, to take possession of the Dekkan. The people fairly believed this, but the case must have been far different amongst themselves, for, as we followed on their track, we passed the skeleton horses they had ridden, footsore and shoeless, their hoofs bound up in rags to protect them from the rough and stony tracks over which they travelled, and shreds of their own ragged clothes hung on the thorns of the wayside bushes; and occasionally we came to an emaciated, wounded, and dying man, whom they had abandoned when closely pressed, and the carrion birds would be circling round him, ready to close in when his eyelids fell in death. It was said a flock of vultures always accompanied their line of march, ready to prey on the men and animals which fell. From Mooltye they took the course of the Taptee valley, and thus drew us into a most unhealthy tract of country, where we were half starved for want of provisions: the few that had existed in the villages they took as they advanced, the inhabitants having left through fear. We had the greatest difficulty in collecting grain for ourselves and horses: after searching the houses, and digging up buried corn, the European soldiery of the force hunted down the young village pigs, and could not be dissuaded from eating them, and we cut the standing jowarree for the cattle.

It was at this time that the Nawab of Banda made the first overture to surrender himself to the Political Agent at Budnoor. An old bearer of the Nawab's brought the letter, and it requested the answer might be sent to a village twenty-five miles distant, and written in the English character, so that it might not be understood if it fell into the hands of Tantia, who now began to mistrust him, and kept his wives, children, and himself under close surveillance. Our force was so much straitened for provisions we could follow no longer the rebel track, and marched on Ellichpoor, and Tantia now endeavoured to get through Sir Hugh Rose's cordon, and enter Candeish; but he met small bodies of troops in every direction, and Brigadier Hill moved out the whole of the Nizam's troops against him, so that he again turned his head for Central India, ran the gauntlet of many forces, and crossed the Nerbudda.

CHAPTER XIII.

TANTIA AND HIS FOLLOWERS RECROSS THE NERBUDDA—MAJOR SUTHERLAND MEETS THEM—BRIGADIER PARKE'S ENGAGEMENT AT OODEPOOR—A SAILOR SEA-SICK—COLONEL BENSON'S ENGAGEMENT NEAR MUNDEESOOR—COLONEL SOMERSET'S ACTION AT BARODE—TANTIA TAKES TO THE DESERT.

THEY did not get over the river, however, without discovery. Major Sutherland, who was on the Agra trunk road, heard of them; and with two hundred Highlanders, mounted on Sarnee camels, and two hundred men of the 4th Regiment, or Bombay Rifle corps, went out to meet them, and saw some of the enemy's sowars in flight. Following their direction he came in sight of Tantia's force on a hill, but it would not stay to fight. Our troops cut up all they could overtake, and the main body fled to Oodepoor, closely followed by Colonel Parke, who caught them here and punished them severely. In this affair a squadron of Cavalry, composed of a troop of H. M.'s 8th Hussars, under Major Clewes, and a troop of the 2nd Bombay Light Cavalry, under Captain Smith, did excellent service, in charging the rebels as they fled past, and, for the first time in Central India, Kerr led the Maharratta Horse into action.

From Oodepoor the enemy passed through the jungles of Banswarra, and it was supposed he intended making a descent on the city of Indore. To prevent this, Colonel Benson with his Cavalry column made one of the best marches on record. He started from his encamping ground twelve miles south of the Nerbudda, crossed the river in boats with the whole of his Cavalry, and made Mhow, a distance of fifty miles, in twenty-six hours. On the 3rd of December the column again left Mhow for Rutlam. Colonel Somerset, who was appointed to command a Cavalry Brigade, joined here, and one march distant from this place a small column was detached under Major Learmouth, of the Lancers, but returned after the expiration of three days, having seen nothing but wandering Bheels, who did our people more harm by their thieving propensities than we inflicted on them. Colonels Benson and Somerset now moved on Pertabghur, twenty-five miles, from whence an order arrived from General Michel, directing Colonel Somerset and his Brigade Major to proceed to Ashta with one hundred and fifty Highlanders on camels, and two Horse Artillery guns, and assume command of a force which was forming there to act against Ferozshah, who, with a large body of Cavalry, was said to have crossed the Ganges, and to be on his way down to effect a junction with Tantia, who was still in the Banswarra jungles. The son of our veteran Commander-in-Chief, and his Brigade Major *en route* to Ashta, passed through Jowra, and shared the hospitalities of the Nawab, who entertains in true English style, even to the beer and champagne. He is fond of, and possesses, good Arab horses, and a collection of rarer animals, such as tigers, cameleopards, lynxes, cheetahs, &c., and here a rather amusing scene presented itself. The Brigade Major volunteered to ride the giraffe, and the Rajah had it brought out barebacked, the bridle consisting simply of a piece of rope round the creature's neck. Vaulting from the balcony on to its back, the Brigade

Major started, at first at a spanking pace, pretty much as Barras's Highlander is represented going in the *Illustrated News*, but when the giraffe attained his gallop, the movement actually induced a sort of sea-sickness in the daring rider, although four years' service in the Navy had rendered him proof against that malady at sea. Until thus affected he rode like a centaur, while the beast's awkward bounds and gyrations caused great merriment. At length down came the rider, who first received a blow on the head from the knee, and then in the face from the giraffe's foot: it seemed to threaten a fatal termination. The Brigade Major was borne away insensible, and did not recover for some hours.

While Colonel Somerset was on his way to Ashta, Colonel Benson still pressed onwards after Tantia, and near Mundeesoor came on the wake of his force, running him hard nearly due east to Zeerapoor. He caught and engaged him, killed a few of his men, and captured seven elephants, with five thousand rupees' worth of silver.

At this time a squadron of the 17th Lancers under Major White, and two hundred men of the 19th Bombay Regiment under Captain

Baugh, left Indore and marched on Deg. Tantia, with Colonel Benson in pursuit, had passed through the place but three hours previous to their arrival. Colonel Somerset having heard Ferozshah's force was insignificant, had turned from it and was close behind, and directed Captain White to join him at Soosneer. This he did, and their combined columns marched on Zeerapoor, arriving there one day after Colonel Benson's engagement with the rebels, and he with his force was still halted there to recruit. At this place intelligence was brought that Ferozshah, in spite of the strong opposition, had effected the junction with Tantia. This induced Colonel Somerset to push on sixteen miles more that night, taking with him two of Colonel Benson's Horse Artillery guns. He halted at Kulchepoor, but at half-past eleven the same night marched again without a rest (save one hour and a half to feed) until half-past 6 the following day, having reached the town of Satul, and then heard the enemy were but ten miles a head. The force again marched at 11 o'clock P. M., and arrived where the rebels were said to be. The road we had traversed was of the worst description, and as it was yet dark we laid down on it until daylight, when a spy came in, reporting the presence of the rebels. We pushed on, and saw their camp-followers under a group of trees. The fighting men had just gone, and a thick cloud of dust indicated the direction. Our Cavalry and Artillery advanced at a trot a distance of seven miles, and, debouching from a village, came on about three thousand of their Cavalry drawn up. They advanced on our guns at a walk, their leader, mounted on a grey horse, appearing to be greatly excited, and endeavouring to animate his men with the same spirit, but the first shot from our guns knocked him over. Some of his followers immediately dismounted, and carried him away, and the remainder, seeing how small was our number, endeavoured to turn our left. Save the escort with the guns, we had but forty or fifty men of the 17th Lancers, a ridiculous handful compared with the enemy, but Major White formed his men in rank entire, and advanced to meet them. It was a pretty sight, and the enemy had so much odds in his favour that it became exciting also. Just at this crisis the Highlanders, who had been scarcely able to keep pace, appeared, and our guns were placed beyond all danger. The fifty Lancers having gone a couple of hundred yards, brought their lances down to the engage, put their horses into a gallop, and with a yell swept down on the rebel Cavalry, which slackened pace, halted, and, when within forty or fifty yards, opened out and fled. Some were speared at once, the rest were pursued seven miles, the killed encumbering the earth with their carcases. Those who owed their escape to the fleetness of their horses, went crashing through the jungle like devils in a whirlwind. The Lancers now returned to Barode, from whence they had started, and encamped there, or rather bivouacked, for the baggage and Commissariat did not come up for eight days afterwards: it had been completely distanced by our rate of marching. Every one was alike badly off: none had tents, and very few any bedding; the soldiers were without tea, arrack, bread, or any of the supplies which the Indian Commissariat Department scarcely ever fails to furnish even under the most disadvantageous circumstances, whether it be on the barren sands of Persia or the devastated tracks in Hindoostan. It was impossible that *impedimenta* could have kept pace in this pursuit. The soldiery knew this, and all cheerfully bore a susbistence on flour and such food as could be obtained in the villages. To add to their discomfort at this time, the nights were exceedingly cold, and it rained heavily for three days and nights in succession. The companies of the Bombay 9th Regiment came up in the evening after the affair, being much exhausted by the continuous marching. A searching party entered the town of Barode and found munitions of war in store for the rebels: there were one hundred and seventy seers of leaden bullets, two hundred seers of gunpowder, a hundred mallets, and thousands of tent-pegs and lamps. An elephant and some prisoners were captured.

From this place the force marched on Chuppra, arriving there about the middle of January. Here we met several of our pursuing columns, which had been ordered to this place by General Michel, who proceeded hence to Boondee. Tantia's force made off to the desert country of Bekaneer: it was doubtful whether he himself accompanied them. Notwithstanding the numerous columns of our troops in the field pursuing him, he seldom deviated from the route he proposed taking, and directed supplies to be stored for him at certain places, and invariably marched through them. Could we but have gained this intelligence, we might have entrapped him, but the supplies were eaten and the arch-rebel gone before we learnt anything connected with it. At Barode a letter was found from a Jalraputtun official, which directed supplies to be laid in for Tantia and his force. It was evidently a document of guilt, as the Vakeel offered the Brigade Major of the force a thousand rupees for it, saying it could be of no service to him. This sum and more was refused. Soon after this the natives played another trick to get possession of it: they robbed his tent of all it contained save his bed and himself, carrying away his clothes, four medals, and a number of *urzees* his moonshee had given him to read, to perfect himself in the Hindoostanee tongue, but the letter had been placed for safe keeping in the field treasure chest, under a sentry, so that they again failed to obtain it.

CHAPTER XIV.

BRIGADIER HONNOR'S NIGHT ATTACK—COLONEL HOLMES' ENGAGEMENT—A BODY OF REBELS SURRENDERS—FIGHTS IN BUNDLEKUND—TANTIA IS BETRAYED AND CAPTURED—TANTIA'S DEATH—ASHES OF THE REBELLION.

TANTIA'S followers did not relish the desert-like aspect of Bikaneer, where starvation threatened them, and they again came rapidly south to the Chutterbooge Pass in the Aravelli range of hills, but were caught by Brigadier Honnor, who killed twenty-five in a night-attack he made, and subsequently Colonel Holmes caught them and killed a like number. They failed to get through the first Pass they attempted, in consequence of the stout resistance offered by a few men of the Mhairwar battalion, but succeeded at the Chutterbooge. Colonel Somerset pursued south, and reached Khonkrowlee after severe marching, on one occasion doing one hundred and twenty miles with scarce a rest even for a few hours; but this pressed the rebels so hard that they fell out by the way, literally exhausted, and preferred meeting their fate to continuing the race for life. During this pursuit Subedar Moideen Khan, with five troopers of the 2nd Bombay Light Cavalry, was detached on the right flank to gain intelligence; he proceeded to Khonkrowlee, and while in the town Tantia's force arrived at the gates; the Subedar had just time enough to close them and attempt an exit at a second gate, but found himself face to face with the rebel sowars; he and his five men at length succeeded in passing free at a third gate and gained the open country, but about one hundred and thirty of the rebel horsemen pursued him for five miles, when the horse of one of the troopers began to show symptoms of distress, and a number of the pursuers had fallen out, none but a few of the best mounted having been able to keep pace. The Subedar seeing this, and that one of his men must speedily be cut up, boldly met the danger, fronted his men and prepared to fight; but the rebel cowards turned away; and Moideen Khan brought his five men into Colonel Somerset's camp the next day, having gone a distance of seventy-two miles; for this service he received the order of Valour. Every means was taken to introduce Her Majesty's Proclamation amongst the rebels, and at Jerun they made overtures to surrender, but each succeeding message demanded more indulgent terms. At this time they were almost surrounded by our various columns, which were halted in order to give their vakeels every inducement to arrange for their surrender, together with their leaders, the Rao and Feroezshah. Tantia Topee was not with them, and report said he had gone to Nepaul. But the small indulgence we gave them was basely taken advantage of, and the main body with their leaders marched across the Agra trunk road into the jungly districts of Nursinghur, while but three hundred men, who had recently joined with Ferozeshah, came over to us. They were not true sepoys, but retainers of Zemindars in Oude, all heartily sick of the sufferings they had undergone. Money was given those that had none, and they were allowed to take away their gaunt and jaded ponies, camels, and horses, and journey to their homes in peace.

Colonel Somerset's force now marched to

Puchore near Sehore, and was broken up ; Colonel de Salis, with various detachments of various corps, early in the month of April marched into the Nursinghur districts to operate against the rebels ; and General Napier came down to Seronge ; whilst Beatson's Horse scoured the jungles in the neighbourhood of Mocksoodonghur. Throughout the whole of the country now infested the roads were mere tracks, horribly stony, and the country so densely covered by vegetation, that it was possible for rebel bands to pass close to our various posts without discovery. The villages were all so small and poverty stricken that they afforded us scanty subsistence only, and the rebels were well nigh destitute of all save life, and their hopes must have been of the faintest description. Scores of them were sick with fever, and Ferozeshah was carried on a common bedstead. Villages were sacked and burnt, and the important men carried away prisoners in order that a sum of money should be paid for their ransom. In the beginning of April they crossed Colonel De Salis' line of baggage, killing a band-master, wounding a sepoy or two, and carried off some beasts of burden; but this force, and also one under Colonel Rich, took its revenge immediately after: they came on the rebels, and one force drove them into the teeth of the other, and cost them a great number of killed, besides dispersing them. Ferozeshah again went north towards Goonah.

From the foregoing narrative it will be seen that after Colonel Somerset's engagement at Barode, Tantia's sun had begun to set, the shadow of that genius of flight had begun to grow less. It was learnt that on one occasion when Tantia and his men marched through a village that belonged to Rajah Maun Singh, before he was proclaimed an out-law by Scindiah, Maun Singh came out to meet Tantia, and was asked to unite his forces with the rebels; but Maun Singh had far too great a respect for English legislature and government to do anything of the kind, and met the offer and solicitations with a stout refusal, on which Tantia made him a prisoner, and it was not without some difficulty Maun Singh effected his escape to the rear of the rebel camp, where a horse awaited him. He was not likely to forget the injury, and, moreover, never at any time was he a bitter enemy to the English. Soon afterwards, when this chief was in treaty with Assistant Quarter Master General Bolton, Tantia again with two followers came for shelter in the territory of his former captive, who, seeing the great advantage to his own cause he should gain by betraying the prince of rebels, cogitated the matter; but the day before he had made his resolve Tantia had left his hiding-place. Maun Singh therefore wrote to Major Meade, and requested that a native officer and fifty sepoys might be placed at his (Maun Singh's) disposal. These he placed in ambush near a hut in a nullah, and sent a servant to call Tantia back to receive an emergent communication. For once the wily Maharatta was deceived, and returned to the appointed place, where Maun Singh met him, and under various pretexts detained him until nightfall, when Tantia and his two servants slept, having yielded to the advice, as it was late. When Maun Singh saw Tantia and his followers sleeping, he gave a preconcerted signal to his servant to call the sepoys from their ambush, and the short time which intervened passed most anxiously with the betrayer; moments seemed as days to him, and he stealthily took Tantia's arms from his person. A few moments more passed in the tortures of suspense, when in rushed the soldiers, and one in his eagerness seized Maun Singh by his long beard, which angered him excessively, till he was released by the order of the subedar. Tantia, seeing at a glance what had happened, said to the Rajah, "What kind of friendship is this?" which elicited a somewhat clever reply from his old prisoner, "I was not previously aware you were my friend." Tantia was now brought a prisoner to Sipree, betraying no fear until he emerged from his palanquin, when he chanced to alight opposite a gin which had been erected for mounting guns. He saw in it all the elements of a gallows which was to remove him from the beautiful earth on which he had played so ignoble a part, and built such a mountain of sorrows, and the despicable wretch showed the pallor of fear as much as his black face could betray it, but again became composed when he was told that he would be allowed a Court Martial to disprove his guilt, if possible. Until the Court assembled he was placed under a guard of Europeans. He made no defence before his tribunal, excepting that in all he had done he had but obeyed the orders of his master the

Nana, who he stated had never given the order for the destruction of our women and children; and in this perversion of the truth he persisted up to the hour of his death. During his trial, when a dependant of Maun Singh's came into court to give evidence against Tantia, stating he was a villager, Tantia asked him, if he was a villager, how it happened that he was present at the battle of the Betwa, which silenced him. The sentence of the court, that he should be hanged, was approved, and on the day the confirmation arrived by telegraph the wretch struggled out of the world, not even having the benefit of a professional hangman; but the death-damps of the grave did not close over him. Tantia will appear again! and not in the vapoury form that Hamlet's father did—not as a spectral illusion, but in the flesh. He is at present in his larva state, and will some day burst his cerements and appear among his fellow-beings again, but it will be in spirit (rectified) and excluded from intercourse with the air of the upper world.

> "Little he deem'd when with his Indian band
> He through the wilds set forth upon his way,"

that such an end was in store for him.

A few of his old companions and followers, the chief of whom are Ferozeshah, the Rao, and Adil Mahommed, are still in the fastnesses of Bundlekund. They are the only live ashes of the rebellion, and blood-red ashes too, and still prefer being hunted like beasts, and living a life of plunder and marauding, to accepting pardon and lands from a graciously-liberal Government. The task of hunting them down is a laborious one, involving long rides in rain or in sunshine, through dense jungles rife with fever, the haunts of wild beasts, not of men. We, to whom the task has fallen, felt much of the spirit of the work had flown when Tantia Topee was no longer to the front, and we care not how hard we work or many we kill so long as we quickly bring to an end the

CENTRAL INDIA CAMPAIGN.